BERLIN

TOP SIGHTS · LOCAL EXPERIENCES

ANDREA SCHULTE-PEEVERS

Contents

Plan Your Trip

Holocaust Memorial (p44)
EDDY GALEOTTI/SHUTTERSTOCK ©

Welcome to Berlin

Berlin is a bon vivant, passionately feasting on the smorgasbord of life. A contagious energy permeates its cafes, bars and clubs, while indie boutiques and progressive restaurants compete for your time with world-class museums and striking landmarks that reflect the city's riveting history. Whether it's must-sees or aimless explorations, Berlin delivers it all in one exciting and memorable package.

View of the Spree River and city skyline

Top Sights

MARIA GOLOVIANKO/SHUTTERSTOCK ©

Reichstag & Government Quarter

Germany's national political power nexus. **p40**

CANADASTOCK/SHUTTERSTOCK ©

Brandenburger Tor
Symbol of division and reunification. **p42**

Pergamonmuseum

A cornucopia of ancient treasures.
p58

Neues Museum

Spotlight on Egypt, Troy and beyond.
p62

Gemäldegalerie

One of world's finest collections of European art. **p72**

Holocaust Memorial

Germany's central Holocaust memorial. **p44**

Schloss Charlottenburg

Berlin's finest Prussian palace ensemble. **p122**

Potsdamer Platz

Architectural showcase of urban renewal. **p76**

Schloss & Park Sanssouci

Royal retreat amid sprawling gardens. **p170**

East Side Gallery

Berlin Wall vestige turned gallery. **p146**

Jüdisches Museum

Jewish-German history in an architectural stunner. **p78**

Gedenkstätte Berliner Mauer

Berlin Wall memorial. **p96**

Eating

Berlin's food scene is growing in leaps and bounds and maturing as beautifully as a fine Barolo. Sure, you can still get your fill of traditional German comfort staples, from sausage to roast pork knuckle, but it's the influx of experimental chefs from around the globe that makes eating in the capital such a delicious and exciting experience.

Modern Regional Cuisine

Healthy eating is sexy, which is why the organic, slow-food and seasonal movements have become an obsession in Berlin. Apple-fed pork from the Havelland, fish from the Müritz Lake District or wild boar from the Schorfheide are becoming quite commonplace on local menus. Some chefs have adopted the 'brutally local' credo and ban any ingredient not grown in the region from their kitchens.

Vegetarian & Vegan

Meat is so last millennium, which is why vegan restaurants are spreading faster than rabbits on Viagra in Berlin. In 2018, Berlin's finest meat-free temple, Cookies Cream (p50), entered the pantheon of Michelin stars.

Local Snacks

A classic Berlin cult snack is the *Curry-wurst*, a fried or grilled *Wiener* sliced into bite-sized ringlets in a spicy tomato sauce and dusted with curry powder. Allegedly invented by a Turkish immigrant in 1970s West Berlin: the Berlin-style doner kebab which features spit-roasted meat slivers tucked into a lightly toasted bread pocket along with salad and a healthy drizzle of yoghurt-based sauces.

Best German

Restaurant am Steinplatz A surprising array of ingredients find their destination in tastebud treats. (p116)

Augustiner am Gendarmenmarkt Go the whole hog at this famous Munich beer-hall transplant. (p50)

Henne No misty-eyed nostalgia, just the ultimate roast chicken, and that since 1907. (p139)

JULIE G WOODHOUSE/ALAMY STOCK PHOTO ©

Schwarzwaldstuben Oldies but goodies from Germany's south amid delightfully irreverent decor. (p103)

Best Fine Dining

Horváth Kreuzberg restaurant dishing up creatively fine-tuned dishes inspired by Austrian cuisine. (p137)

Tulus Lotrek Feel-good fine dining with aroma-rich feasts and superb wines. (p137)

Schwein Elevated nose-to-tail cuisine with stunning wine and gin selections. (p116)

Best Vegetarian

Cookies Cream Clandestine Michelin kitchen tiptoes between hip and haute. (p50)

Vöner Berlin's vegan doner pioneer. (p153)

Best Asian

Umami Sharp Indochine nosh for fans of the classics and the innovative amid sensuous lounge decor. (pictured above; p165)

Zenkichi Japanese morsels for the soul in a sophisticated *izakaya* with sake sommelier. (p102)

Kin Dee Top Thai parlour for modern and localised spins on the classics. (p87)

Best Middle Eastern

Yafo Vibrant Tel Aviv-style haunt with luscious food and great cocktails. (p165)

Koshary Lux Snack place specialising in perky street food from Morocco to Yemen. (p114)

Top Tips for Eating

○ Reservations are essential at top eateries and recommended for midrange places.

○ Your bill won't be presented until you ask for it: 'Zahlen, bitte.'

○ It's customary to add 10% for good service.

Drinking & Nightlife

As one of Europe's primo party playgrounds, Berlin offers a thousand and one scenarios for getting your cocktails and kicks (or wine or beer, for that matter). From cocktail lairs and concept bars, craft beer pubs to rooftop lounge, the next thirst parlour is usually within stumbling distance.

Club Scene

What distinguishes the Berlin scene from those of other party capitals is its focus on independent, non-mainstream niche venues, run by owners or collectives with a creative rather than a corporate background. The shared goal is to usually promote a diverse, inclusive and progressive club culture rather than to maximize profit. At top clubs, though, doors can be tough as staff strive to sift out people that would feel uncomfortable with the music, the vibe or the libertine ways past the door.

When to Go

Berlin's famously long nights have gotten even later of late and, thanks to a growing number of after parties and daytime clubs, not going home until Monday night is definitely an option at weekends. In fact, truly savvy clubbers put in a good night's sleep, then hit the dance floor when other people might head for Sunday church or afternoon tea.

Best Craft-Beer Pubs

Hopfenreich Berlin's first craft-beer bar also has tastings, tap takeovers and guest brewers. (p142)

BrewDog Trendy spot with 30 taps dispensing its Town and guest drafts. (p168)

Hops & Barley Unfiltered pilsner, dark and wheat beer poured in a former butcher's shop. (p156)

Best Cocktail Bars

Bar am Steinplatz Supreme libations in this classy hotel den. (p117)

Buck & Breck Cocktail classics for grown-ups in a speakeasy-style setting. (p105)

ADAM EASTLAND/ALAMY STOCK PHOTO ©

Thelonius Neukölln drinking reaches new heights amid soft sounds, lovely light and expert cocktails. (p133)

Best Beer Gardens

Prater Garten Berlin's oldest beer garden still rocks beneath the chestnuts after 175 years in business. (p166)

BRLO Brwhouse Local craft beer giant with beer garden spilling over into vast Park am Gleisdreieck. (p90)

Schleusenkrug Sprawling, classic joint sitting pretty next to a canal lock on the edge of the Tiergarten park. (p116)

Best Rooftop Bars

Klunkerkranich Hipster spot with urban garden and great sunset views atop a Neukölln shopping centre. (pictured above; p133)

House of Weekend Club-affiliate delivers cocktails and barbecue at eye level with Fernsehturm (TV Tower). (p68)

Best Clubs

Berghain/Panorama Bar Big, bad Berghain is still the best in town. (p154)

://about blank Gritty techno hot spot with an enchanting summer garden. (p155)

Club der Visionäre Outdoor spot on an idyllic canal, popular for day-to-night-to-day partying. (p140)

Top Clubbing Tips

○ Fancy labels and glam cocktail dresses can actually get in the way of your getting in. Wear something black and casual.

○ Be respectful in the queue, don't drink and don't talk too loudly. Don't arrive wasted.

Shopping

Berlin is a great place to shop, and we're definitely not talking malls and chains. The city's appetite for the individual manifests in small neighbourhood boutiques and buzzing markets that are a pleasure to explore. Shopping here is as much about visual stimulus as it is about actually spending your cash.

Where to Shop

Berlin's main shopping boulevard is Kurfürstendamm (Ku'damm) in the City West and Charlottenburg, which is largely the purview of mainstream retailers (from H&M to Prada). Its extension, Tauentzienstrasse, is anchored by KaDeWe, continental Europe's largest department store. Standouts among the city's dozens of other shopping centres are the concept mall Bikini Berlin and the vast LP12 Mall of Berlin at Leipziger Platz.

Getting the most out of shopping in Berlin, though, means venturing off the high street and into the *Kieze* (neighbourhoods). This is where you'll discover a cosmopolitan cocktail of indie boutiques stirred by the city's zest for life, envelope-pushing energy and entrepreneurial spirit.

Opening Hours

Malls, department stores and supermarkets open from 9.30am to 8pm or 9pm; some supermarkets are 24 hours. Boutiques and other smaller shops have flexible hours, usually from 11am to 7pm weekdays, and to 4pm or 5pm Saturday. Stores are closed on Sunday, except for some bakeries, flower shops, souvenir shops, and supermarkets in major train stations, including Hauptbahnhof, Friedrichstrasse and Ostbahnhof.

Best Shopping Areas

Kurfürstendamm
Quintessential high-street shopping along with indie boutiques in the side streets. (p119)

UGIS RIBA/SHUTTERSTOCK ©

Scheunenviertel Edgy local and international labels in chic boutiques and concept stores around Hackescher Markt. (p107)

Kreuzberg & Neukölln Vintage fashion and streetwear along with music and accessories, all in indie boutiques. (p143)

Flea Markets

Flohmarkt im Mauerpark The mother of all Berlin markets is overrun but still a good show. (p161)

Nowkoelln Flowmarkt International hipster market and showcase of local creativity. (p143)

RAW Flohmarkt Major bargains are there for the taking amid lovably ramshackle flair. (p157)

Best Malls & Department Stores

Bikini Berlin Renovated 1950s landmark building with hip stores and views of the monkeys at Zoo Berlin. (pictured above; p120)

LP12 Mall of Berlin Huge high-end shopping quarter with 270 stores alongside apartments, a hotel and offices. (p91)

KaDeWe The largest department store in continental Europe. (p119)

Best Culinary Delights

KaDeWe Food Hall Mindboggling bonanza of gourmet treats from around the world. (p119)

Markthalle Neun Revitalised historic market hall with thrice-weekly farmers market and global bites during Street Food Thursday. (p143)

Bonbonmacherei Willy Wonka would feel right at home in this old-fashioned candy kitchen. (p107)

Türkischer Markt Bazaarlike canal-side market with bargain-priced produce and Mediterranean deli fare. (p133)

Best Bookshops

Dussmann – Das Kulturkaufhaus Vast literature and music emporium with extended shopping hours. (p55)

Museums

With more museums than rainy days (around 170 at last count), Berlin has an extraordinarily diverse cultural landscape that caters for just about every interest, be it art, film, history, nature, computers, antiquities or even Currywurst (a local snack). Many of them are considered must-see attractions – and not just on rainy days.

Museum Island

Museum Island (Museumsinsel), a Unesco World Heritage site, presents 6000 years of art and cultural history in five massive repositories. Marvel at antiquities at the Pergamonmuseum and Altes Museum, meet Egyptian queen Nefertiti at the Neues Museum, take in 19th-century art at the Alte Nationalgalerie and admire medieval sculptures at the Bode-Museum.

History Museums

From its humble medieval beginnings, Berlin's history – and especially its key role in major events of the 20th century – is a rich and endlessly fascinating tapestry. It's also extremely well documented and easily discovered, in numerous museums, memorial sites and monuments, many of them in original historic locations and most of them free.

Nationalgalerie Berlin

The National Gallery is a top-ranked collection of mostly European art from the 19th century to today. The Alte Nationalgalerie specialises in neoclassical, romantic, impressionist and early modernist art; at the Hamburger Bahnhof the spotlight is on international contemporary art; the Museum Berggruen focuses on Picasso; and the Sammlung Scharf-Gerstenberg on surrealist art.

ELENA FAHRO/SHUTTERSTOCK ©

Best History Museums

Deutsches Historisches Museum Comprehensive journey through 2000 years of Germany's turbulent past. (pictured above; p48)

Jüdisches Museum Goes beyond the Holocaust in tracing the history of Jews in Germany. (p78)

DDR Museum Engaging look at daily life behind the Iron Curtain. (p65)

Best Niche Museums

Bröhan Museum Objects and furniture from the art deco, art nouveau and functionalist periods. (p124)

Museum für Naturkunde Meet giant dinos in Berlin's own 'Jurassic Park'. (p100)

Museum für Film und Fernsehen An entertaining romp through German celluloid history. (p77)

Best for Antiquities

Pergamonmuseum Treasure trove of monumental architecture from ancient civilisations. (p58)

Altes Museum Gorgeous Schinkel building sheltering priceless antique art and sculpture. (p66)

Neues Museum Pay your respects to Queen Nefertiti and her entourage. (p62)

Worth a Trip

The original Checkpoint Charlie guard cabin and a reconstructed spy tunnel are among the exhibits at the **Allied Museum** (Allied Museum; ☎030-818 1990; www.alliiertenmuseum.de; Clayallee 135; admission free; ⊙10am-6pm Tue-Sun; P; UOskar-Helene-Heim), which documents historic milestones and the challenges faced by the Western Allies during the Cold War. It's in the southwestern suburb of Grunewald.

Architecture

After visiting the German capital in 1891, Mark Twain remarked, 'Berlin is the newest city I've ever seen'. True then, still true now. Destruction and division have ensured that today's city is essentially a creation of modern times, a showcase of 20th-century styles with few surviving vestiges of earlier times.

Post-Reunification

The fall of the Wall in 1989 presented Berlin with both the challenge and the opportunity to redefine itself architecturally. Huge gashes of empty space opened where the city's halves were to be rejoined. The grandest of the post-1990 developments is Potsdamer Platz, a contemporary interpretation of the famous historic square. Other architectural standouts include the Bundeskanzleramt (Federal Chancellery), the Jüdisches Museum and the Neues Museum.

The Schinkel Touch

The architectural style that most shaped Berlin was neoclassicism, thanks in large part to one man: Karl Friedrich Schinkel (1781–1841), arguably Prussia's most prominent architect. His first solo commission was the Neue Wache but the nearby Altes Museum is considered his most mature work.

The 1920s & Bauhaus

The spirit of innovation brought some of the finest avant-garde architects to Berlin in the 1920s, including Le Corbusier, Ludwig Mies van der Rohe and Hans Scharoun. Their association later evolved into the Bauhaus, which used practical anti-elitist principles to unite form and function and had a profound effect on modern aesthetics.

Best of Schinkel

Altes Museum The grand colonnaded front inspired by a philosopher's school

POSZTOS/SHUTTERSTOCK ©

in Athens is considered Schinkel's most mature work. (p66)

Konzerthaus Berlin A sweeping staircase leads to a raised columned portico in this famous concert hall. (p54)

Neue Wache This royal guardhouse turned antiwar memorial was Schinkel's first Berlin commission. (p49)

Best Post-WWII Modernism

Berliner Philharmonie This eccentric concert hall is Hans Scharoun's modernist masterpiece. (p91)

Haus der Kulturen der Welt Avant-garde structure with gravity-defying sculptural roof. (p48)

Best Contemporary

Jüdisches Museum Daniel Libeskind's zigzagshaped architectural metaphor for Jewish history. (p78)

Neues Museum David Chipperfield's reconstructed New Museum ingeniously blends old and new. (p62)

Sony Center Helmut Jahn's svelte glass-and-steel complex is the most striking building on Potsdamer Platz. (pictured above; p77)

Worth a Trip

Built for the 1936 Olympic Games, Berlin's coliseum-style **Olympiastadion** (Olympic Stadium; ☎030-2500 2322; https://olympia stadion.berlin; Olympischer Platz 3; adult/concession self-guided tour €8/5.50, highlights tour €11/9.50; ⏰9am-7pm Apr-Jul, Sep & Oct, to 8pm Aug, 10am-4pm Nov-Mar; Ⓢ Olympia-stadion, Ⓤ Olympiastadion) was revamped for the 2006 FIFA World Cup and now sports a spidery oval roof, snazzy VIP boxes and top sound, lighting and projection systems.

Historical Sites

In Berlin the past is always present. Strolling along boulevards and around neighbourhoods, you can't help but pass legendary sights that take you back to the era of Prussian glory, the dark ages of the Third Reich, the tense period of the Cold War and the euphoria of reunification.

The Age of Prussia

Berlin has been a royal residence since 1701 when Elector Friedrich III was elevated to King Friedrich I. This promotion significantly shaped the city, which blossomed under Frederick the Great, who sought greatness as much on the battlefield as through building. In the 19th century, Prussia weathered revolutions and industrialisation to forge the creation of the German Reich, which lasted until the monarchy's demise in 1918.

The Third Reich

No other political power shaped the 20th century as much as Nazi Germany. The megalomania of Hitler and his henchmen wrought destruction upon much of Europe, bringing death to at least 50 million people, and forever realigned the world order. Few original sites remain, but memorials and museums keep the horror in focus.

Cold Wall Chills

After WWII, Germany fell into the crosshairs of the Cold War as a country divided along ideological lines by the victorious powers, its internal border marked by fences and a wall. Just how differently the two countries developed is still palpable in Berlin, expressed not only through Berlin Wall remnants such as the East Side Gallery but also through vastly different urban planning and architectural styles.

PHOTOCREO MICHAL BEDNAREK/SHUTTERSTOCK ©

Best of Prussian Pomp

Brandenburger Tor Germany's most iconic national symbol. (p42)

Reichstag Palatial home of the German parliament. (pictured above; p40)

Schloss Charlottenburg Sumptuous palace provides a glimpse into the lifestyles of the rich and royal. (p122)

Berliner Dom Royal court church with impressive dimensions, stunning acoustics and fanciful sarcophagi. (p66)

Best of Cold War Berlin

Gedenkstätte Berliner Mauer Indoor-outdoor exhibit illustrates the history, physical appearance and social impact of the Berlin Wall. (p96)

East Side Gallery The longest remaining stretch of Berlin Wall turned art canvas by more than 100 artists. (p146)

Karl-Marx-Allee East Berlin's pompous yet impressive main boulevard and showpiece of socialist architecture. (p150)

Best of WWII History

Topographie des Terrors Gripping examination of the origins of Nazism, its perpetrators and its victims, on the site of the SS and Gestapo headquarters. (p85)

Holocaust Memorial Commemorates the unspeakable horrors of the WWII Jewish genocide. (p44)

Art

Art aficionados will find their compass on perpetual spin in Berlin. Home to hundreds of galleries, scores of world-class collections and some 33,000 international artists, it has assumed a pole position on the global artistic circuit.

Commercial Art Galleries

The **Galleries Association of Berlin** (www.berliner-galerien.de) counts some 400 galleries within the city. In addition, there are at least 200 noncommercial showrooms and off-spaces that regularly show new exhibitions. Although the orientation is global, it's well worth keeping an eye out for the latest works by major contemporary artists living and working in Berlin, including Thomas Demand, Jonathan Meese, Via Lewandowsky, Isa Genzken, Tino Sehgal, Esra Ersen, John Bock and the artist duo Ingar Dragset and Michael Elmgreen.

Galleries cluster in four main areas: along Auguststrasse and Linienstrasse in the Scheunenviertel; around Checkpoint Charlie (eg Zimmerstrasse, Markgrafenstrasse); on Potsdamer Strasse in Schöneberg; and around Savignyplatz near Kurfürstendamm.

Public Art

Free installations, sculptures and paintings? Absolutely. Public art is big in Berlin, which happens to be home to the world's longest outdoor mural, the 1.3km-long East Side Gallery (p146). No matter which neighbourhood you walk in, you're going to encounter public art on a grand scale.

Best Old Masters

Gemäldegalerie Sweeping survey of six centuries of canvas candy from Germany, Italy, France, Spain and the Netherlands. (p72)

JANNIS WERNER/ALAMY STOCK PHOTO ©

Alte Nationalgalerie Showcase of 19th-century art by leading German romantics and realists. (p66)

Best Niche Collections

Museum Berggruen Priceless Picassos, plus works by Klee and Giacometti. (p124)

Sammlung Scharf-Gerstenberg Enter the surreal worlds conjured up by Goya, Max Ernst, Magritte and other giants of the genre. (p124)

Best Contemporary Art

Hamburger Bahnhof Legends like Warhol, Beuys and Twombly are aboard the contemporary-art express at this former train station. (p100)

Sammlung Boros Book months ahead for tickets to see this cutting-edge private collection in a WWII bunker. (p100)

Best Street Art

Haus Schwarzenberg Awesome works on courtyard facades of this hub of subculture. (p102)

RAW Gelände Constantly evolving canvas with dedicated street art gallery called Urban Spree. (pictured above; p156)

Skalitzer Strasse & Around Lots of small- and large-scale street art. In Kreuzberg. (p128)

Tours

If you're a Berlin first-timer, letting someone else show you around is a great way to get your bearings, see the key sights quickly and obtain a general understanding of the city. All manner of explorations – from generic city bus tours to special-interest outings – are available.

Walking & Cycling Tours

Several companies offer English-language general city explorations and themed tours (eg Third Reich, Cold War, Potsdam) that don't require reservations – you just show up at the designated meeting point. Since these may change, check online for the latest or look for flyers in hotel or hostel lobbies. Some guides work for tips only but the better tours cost between €12 and €20 and run three to five hours.

Boat Tours

On a warm day, it's fun to see Berlin from the deck of a boat cruising the city's rivers, canals and lakes. Tours range from one-hour spins around the historic centre to longer trips to Schloss Charlottenburg and beyond. Most operators offer live commentary in English and German and sell refreshments on board. Embarkation points are around Museum Island; check the website of **Stern und Kreisschiffahrt** (☏030-536 3600; www. sternundkreis.de; tours from €15; ⏰Mar-Dec) for other locations.

Best Cycling & Walking Tours

Alternative Berlin Tours (☏0162 819 8264; www.alternativeberlin.com; tours €12-35) Roster includes tip-based subculture tours, a street-art tour and workshop, an alternative pub crawl and a craft-beer tour.

Berlin on Bike (☏030-4373 9999; www.berlinon bike.de; Knaackstrasse 97, Kulturbrauerei, Court 4; tours incl bike adult/concession €24/20, bike rental per 24hr €10; ⏰8am-8pm mid-Mar–mid-Nov, 10am-4pm Mon-Sat mid-Nov–mid-Mar; 🚊M1, Ⓤ Eberswalder Strasse) Daily city and Berlin Wall tours along with Alternative Berlin and Street Art tours.

Original Berlin Walks (☏030-301 9194; www.

berlinwalks.de; adult/concession from €14/12) Berlin's longest-running English-language walking tour company has a large roster of general and themed tours.

Brewer's Berlin Tours

(📞0177 388 1537; www.brewersberlintours.com; adult/concession €15/12) Epic six-hour city tour plus themed tours on craft beer, spies and Potsdam.

Best Speciality Tours

Berliner Unterwelten

(📞030-4991 0517; www.berliner-unterwelten.de; Brunnenstrasse 105; adult/concession €12/10; ⏱Dark Worlds tours in English 11am Wed-Sun year-round, 3pm Mon, Wed-Sun, 1pm Wed-Sun Apr-

Oct; Ⓢ Gesundbrunnen, Ⓤ Gesundbrunnen) Get a look at Berlin from below as you explore a dark and dank subterranean WWII air-raid shelter.

Green Me Berlin Tours

(www.greenmeberlin.com; public tours per person €30-50, private tours on request) Insider walking tours take you behind the scenes of Berlin's active and creative eco and sustainability scenes.

Eat the World (📞030-206 229 990; www.eat-the-world.com; tours €33)

Three-hour culinary sightseeing tours with stops at cafes, delis, bakeries and more.

Trabi Safari (📞030-3020 1030; www.trabi-safari.de; Zimmerstrasse 97; adult/child under 17 from €49/free; Ⓤ Kochstrasse)

Turn the clock back while driving yourself around the city in an original East German Trabant car.

Top Tip for Tours

Get a crash course in 'Berlin-ology' by hopping on public bus 100 or 200 at Zoologischer Garten or Alexanderplatz and letting the sights whoosh by for the price of an AB transport ticket.

Quiet Spots

D.BOND/SHUTTERSTOCK ©

If your head is spinning with all the stimulus Berlin is throwing at you, there are plenty of places that can provide a restorative antidote. Fantastic outdoor spots and serene retreats await in every neighbourhood.

Best Parks & Gardens

Schlossgarten Charlottenburg Set up a picnic near the carp pond and ponder royal splendours. (p123)

Tiergarten Take pleasure in getting lost amid the lawns, trees and paths of one of the world's largest city parks. (p80)

Park Sanssouci Find your favourite spot away from the crowds in this sprawling royal park. (p170)

Volkspark Friedrichshain Expansive 'people's park' with hills created from WWII rubble. (p150)

Best Memorial Sites

Holocaust Memorial An outsized maze of stelae represents this outsized crime against humanity. (pictured above; p44)

Luftbrückendenkmal Pay tribute to a true triumph of the will' at the Berlin Airlift Memorial. (p93)

Neue Wache An antiwar memorial centred on an emotional Käthe Kollwitz sculpture. (p49)

Best Churches

Berliner Dom Royal court church cutting a commanding presence on Museum Island. (p66)

Kaiser-Wilhelm-Gedächtniskirche Bombed-out church serves as poignant reminder of the futility of war. (p112)

For Kids

Travelling to Berlin with kids can be child's play, especially if you keep a light schedule and involve them in day-to-day planning. There's plenty to do to keep youngsters occupied, from zoos to kid-oriented museums. Parks and imaginative playgrounds abound in all neighbourhoods, as do public pools.

ANTICICLO/SHUTTERSTOCK ©

Legoland Discovery Centre (pictured above; ☎01806-6669 0110; www.legolanddiscoverycentre.de/berlin; Potsdamer Strasse 4; €19.50; ⏲10am-7pm, last admission 5pm; 🚌200, Ⓢ Potsdamer Platz, Ⓤ Potsdamer Platz) The milk-tooth set delights in this Lego wonderland with rides, entertainment and interactive stations.

Deutsches Technikmuseum (German Museum of Technology; ☎030-902 540; http://sdtb.de/technikmuseum; Trebbiner Strasse 9; adult/concession/child under 18 €8/4/after 3pm free; ⏲9am-5.30pm Tue-Fri, 10am-6pm Sat & Sun; Ⓟ🚹; Ⓤ Gleisdreieck, Möckernbrücke) This vast shrine to technology is packed with discoveries,

including the world's first computer, an entire hall of vintage locomotives and exhibits on aerospace and navigation in a modern annexe.

Science Center Spectrum (☎030-9025 4284; www.sdtb.de; Möckernstrasse 26; adult/concession/child under 18 €8/4/free after 3pm; ⏲9am-5.30pm Tue-Fri, 10am-6pm Sat & Sun; Ⓟ; Ⓤ Möckernbrücke, Gleisdreieck) Play with, experience and learn about such things as balance, weight, water, air and electricity in dozens of hands-on science experiments.

Tierpark Berlin (☎030-515 310; www.tierpark-berlin.de; Am Tierpark 125; adult/concession/child 4-15yr €14/9/7; ⏲zoo

9am-6.30pm Apr-Sep, to 6pm Mar & Oct, to 4.30pm Nov-Feb, palace 11am-6pm Tue-Sun Apr-Oct, to 4.30pm Nov-Mar; Ⓟ🚹; Ⓤ Tierpark) Expect plenty of ooh and aah moments when kids watch baby elephants at play or see lions and tigers being fed at this vast animal park.

Sealife Berlin (☎0180-666 690 101; www.visitsealife.com; Spandauer Strasse 3; adult/child €18/14.50, cheaper online; ⏲10am-7pm, last admission 6pm; 🚌100, 200, TXL, Ⓢ Hackescher Markt, Alexanderplatz) Little ones get to press their noses against dozens of fish-filled tanks, solve puzzles and admire starfish and sea anemones up close.

LGBT+

Berlin's legendary liberalism has spawned one of the world's biggest, most divine and diverse LGBT+ playgrounds. Anything goes in 'Homopolis' (and we do mean anything!), from the highbrow to the hands-on, the bourgeois to the bizarre, the mainstream to the flamboyant.

Community

The area around Nollendorfplatz (Motzstrasse and Fuggerstrasse especially) has been a gay mecca since the 1920s. Institutions like Heile Welt, Tom's, Connection and Hafen pull in the punters night after night, and there's also plenty of nocturnal action for the leather and fetish set. The crowd skews younger, wilder and more alternative around Kottbusser Tor and along Oranienstrasse where key venues stay open till sunrise and beyond. For a DIY subcultural vibe, head across the canal to Neukölln. Things are comparatively subdued in the bars and cafes along main-strip Mehringdamm. Friedrichshain is a de rigueur stop on the gay nightlife circuit thanks to clubs like Berghain, the hands-on Lab.oratory, Suicide Circus and :// about blank.

Partying

Generally speaking, Berlin's gayscape runs the entire spectrum from mellow cafes, campy bars and cinemas to saunas, cruising areas, clubs with darkrooms and all-out sex venues. In fact, sex and sexuality are entirely everyday matters to the unshockable city folks and there are very few, if any, itches that can't be quite openly and legally scratched. As elsewhere, gay men have more options for having fun, but grrrrls of all stripes won't feel left out either.

Best Weekly Parties

GMF (www.gmf-berlin.de; Alexanderstrasse 7; entry €12; ⏰11pm Sun; Ⓤ Alexanderplatz, Ⓢ Alexanderplatz)

Berlin's premier techno-house Sunday club, currently taking place at House of Weekend.

Chantals House of Shame (www.facebook. com/ChantalsHouseof Shame; Revaler Strasse 99, Suicide Circus; ☺11pm-8am Thu; 🚊M10, M13, Ⓤ Warschauer Platz, Ⓢ Warschauer Platz) Eponymous trash-drag diva's Thursday party at Suicide Circus runs wild and wicked.

Cafe Fatal (http://so36. de; Oranienstrasse 190; ☺7pm-late Sun; Ⓤ Kottbusser Tor) All comers descend on SO36 for the ultimate rainbow Sunday tea dance (from 7pm), which goes from 'strictly ballroom' to 'dirty dancing' in a flash.

Best Bars

Heile Welt (☎030-2191 7507; Motzstrasse 5; ☺7pm-3am; Ⓤ Nollendorfplatz) Stylish lounge good for mingling over cocktails.

Zum Schmutzigen Hobby (☎030-3646 8446; www.facebook.com/zum schmutzigenhobby; Revaler Strasse 99, RAW Gelände, Gate 2; ☺7.30pm-late; 🚊M10, M13, Ⓢ Warschauer Strasse, Ⓤ Warschauer Strasse) Fabulously wacky party pen in a former fire station.

Himmelreich (☎030-2936 9292; www. himmelreich-berlin.de; Simon-Dach-Strasse 36; ☺6pm-2am or later Mon-Sat, 4pm-1am or later Sun; 🚊M13, M10, Ⓢ Warschauer Strasse, Ⓤ Warschauer Strasse) '50s retro lounge is

a lesbigay-scene stalwart in Friedrichshain.

Rauschgold (☎030-9227 4178; www.rauschgold.berlin; Mehringdamm 62; ☺8pm-late; 📶; Ⓤ Mehringdamm) Glitter-glam bar for all-night fun with pop, karaoke and drag shows.

Best Clubs

SchwuZ (☎030-5770 2270; www.schwuz. de; Rollbergstrasse 26; ☺11pm-late Thu-Sat; 🚊104, 167, Ⓤ Rathaus Neukölln) LGBTIQ club with different parties – great for scene newbies.

Lab.oratory (pictured above; www.lab-oratory. de; Am Wriezener Bahnhof; ☺Thu-Sun; Ⓢ Ostbahnhof) Fetish-oriented experimental play zone in industrial setting below Berghain.

Four Perfect Days

Day 1

MIBIRDY/GETTY IMAGES ©

One day in Berlin? Check off the key sights on this whirlwind itinerary. Book ahead for access to the **Reichstag** (pictured; p40) dome, then snap a picture of the **Brandenburg Gate** (p42) before exploring the maze of the **Holocaust Memorial** (p44) and admiring the contemporary architecture of **Potsdamer Platz** (p76).

Head to **Checkpoint Charlie** (p85) and saunter over to glorious **Gendarmenmarkt** (p48) square and lunch at **Augustiner am Gendarmenmarkt** (p50). Head east on Unter den Linden to spend the afternoon at the **Pergamonmuseum** (p58).

Wind down over dinner at **Katz Orange** (p102) and dancing at **Clärchens Ballhaus** (p105).

Day 2

CANADASTOCK/SHUTTERSTOCK ©

Start the day by coming to grips with life in Berlin when the Wall still stood at the **Gedenkstätte Berliner Mauer** (p96). Poke around the boutiques on Kastanienallee before grabbing lunch at **W-Der Imbiss** (p166).

In the afternoon, pay respects to Queen Nefertiti and other treasures at the engrossing **Neues Museum** (p62) followed by a chill one-hour **river cruise** (pictured) around Museumsinsel. Enjoy a cocktail TV Tower views from the **House of Weekend** (p68) rooftop bar.

Head to Kreuzberg for dinner at **Orania** (p136), then follow up with a bar-hop around Kottbusser Tor, with cocktails at **Würgeengel** (p131), beer at **Möbel Olfe** (p131) or wine at **Otto Rink** (p131).

Day 3

KIEV.VICTOR/SHUTTERSTOCK ©

Kick the day off at **Schloss Charlottenburg** (p122), where the **Neuer Flügel** (New Wing) is an essential stop. Meditate upon the futility of war at the **Kaiser-Wilhelm-Gedächtniskirche** (p112), then – assuming it's not Sunday – satisfy your shopping cravings along **Kurfürstendamm** (p119) capped by lunch in the **KaDeWe** (pictured; p119) food hall.

Swing by the striking Libeskind-designed **Jüdisches Museum** (p78), then head down to **Tempelhofer Feld** (p129) to see how an old airport can be recycled into a sustainable park and playground. Have a break in the park's beer garden.

Wrap up the day with dinner at **eins44** (p138) followed by a bar hop along **Weserstrasse** and side streets.

Day 4

UGIS RIBA/SHUTTERSTOCK ©

Leave the city behind on a saunter around the parks and palaces in Potsdam, a mere 40-minute *S-Bahn* ride away. Book time-slot online tickets for **Schloss Sanssouci** (p171), a jewel of a palace, then explore the surrounding park and its many palaces, including the **Chinesisches Haus** (p171).

Head into Potsdam's old town and the **Holländisches Viertel** (Dutch Quarter; pictured) or marvel at top-notch art in the dashing **Museum Barberini** (p173) before heading back to Berlin for post-sightseeing mugs at **Prater** (p166) beer garden.

Pull up a stool at Prenzlauer Berg's buzzy **Umami** (p165) for modern Vietnamese fare, then sip a nightcap cocktail at **Bryk Bar** (p167) or **Becketts Kopf** (p168).

Need to Know

For detailed information, see Survival Guide (p175)

Currency
Euro (€)

Language
German

Visas
Generally not required for tourist stays of up to 90 days (or at all for EU nationals); some nationalities need a Schengen visa.

Money
ATMs widespread. Cash is king; credit card acceptance is growing, but don't count on it.

Time
Clocks in Germany are set to central European time (GMT/UTC plus one hour). Daylight-savings time kicks in on the last Sunday in March and ends on the last Sunday in October.

Tipping
Servers 10%, bartenders 5%, taxi drivers 10%, porters €1 to €2 per bag, room cleaners €1 to €2 per day, toilet attendants €0.50.

Daily Budget

Budget: Less than €100
Dorm bed or peer-to-peer rental: €18–35
Doner kebab: €3–4
Club cover: €5–15
Public transport day pass: €7

Midrange: €100–200
Private apartment or double room: €80–120
Two-course dinner with wine: €40–60
Guided tour: €10–20
Museum admission: €8–20

Top end: More than €200
Upmarket apartment or double in top-end hotel: from €180
Gourmet two-course dinner with wine: €80
Cabaret ticket: €50–80
Taxi ride: €25

Advance Planning

Two to three months before Book tickets for the Berliner Philharmonie, the Staatsoper, Sammlung Boros and top-flight events.

One month before Reserve a table at trendy or Michelin-starred restaurants, especially for Friday and Saturday dinners.

Two weeks before Book online tickets for the Reichstag dome, the Neues Museum and the Pergamonmuseum.

Arriving in Berlin

✈ Tegel Airport

TXL express bus to Alexanderplatz (40 minutes) and bus X9 for City-West (eg Zoo station, 20 minutes), €2.80; taxi €25 to €25.

✈ Schönefeld Airport

Airport-Express trains (RB14 or RE7) to central Berlin twice hourly (30 minutes), and S9 trains every 20 minutes for Friedrichshain and Prenzlauer Berg, €3.40; taxi to city centre €45 to €50.

🚆 Hauptbahnhof

Main train station in the city centre; served by S-Bahn, U-Bahn, tram, bus and taxi.

🚆 Zentraler Omnibus Bahnhof

The central bus station is in the city's west. U-Bahn U2 to city centre (eg Bahnhof Zoo, eight minutes; Alexanderplatz, 28 minutes), €2.80; taxi €14 to CityWest, €24 to Alexanderplatz.

Getting Around

Ⓤ U-Bahn

Most efficient way to travel; operates 4am to 12.30am and all night Friday, Saturday and public holidays. From Sunday to Thursday, half-hourly night buses take over in the interim.

Ⓢ S-Bahn

Less frequent than U-Bahn trains but with fewer stops; useful for longer distances. Same operating hours as the U-Bahn.

🚌 Bus

Slow but useful for sightseeing on the cheap. Run frequently 4.30am to 12.30am; half-hourly night buses in the interim. MetroBuses (designated eg M1, M19) operate 24/7.

🚋 Tram

Only in the eastern districts; Metro-Trams (eg M1, M2) run 24/7.

NITO/SHUTTERSTOCK ©

Berlin Neighbourhoods

Scheunenviertel (p95)
The maze-like historic Jewish Quarter is fashionista central and also teems with hip bars and restaurants.

Schloss Charlottenburg

Reichstag & Government Quarter

Brandenburger Tor
Holocaust Memorial
Gemäldegalerie

Potsdamer Platz

Kurfürstendamm & City West (p109)
Nirvana for shopaholics, this grand boulevard spills into idyllic side streets teeming with quaint shops, bustling cafes and restaurants.

Potsdamer Platz (p71)
Built in the 1990s on ground once bisected by the Berlin, this quarter is a showcase of fabulous contemporary architecture.

Reichstag & Unter Den Linden (p39)
Berlin's historic hub delivers great views, iconic landmarks and the city's most beautiful boulevard.

Prenzlauer Berg (p159)
This charismatic neighbourhood entices with fun shopping, gorgeous townhouses, cosy cafes and a fabulous flea market.

Gedenkstätte Berliner Mauer

Pergamonmuseum

Neues Museum

Museum Island & Alexanderplatz (p57)
Gawk at a pirate's chest of treasure from ancient civilisations guarded by the soaring TV Tower on socialist-styled Alexanderplatz.

Jüdisches Museum

East Side Gallery

Kreuzberg & Neukölln (p129)
Gritty but cool, Kreuzberg and Neukölln are a joy to explore on foot, with vibrant restaurant scenes and Berlin's most happening nightlife.

Friedrichshain (p145)
This student-flavoured district is tailor-made for soaking up Berlin's laid-back vibe and great for nightlife explorations.

Explore
Berlin

Worth a Trip 👀

Berlin's Walking Tours 🚶

Clärchens Ballhaus (p105) ROGER CRACKNELL 01/CLASSIC/ALAMY STOCK PHOTO ©

Explore ◉

Reichstag & Unter Den Linden

It's been burned, bombed, rebuilt, buttressed by the Berlin Wall, wrapped in fabric and, finally, adorned with a glass dome: the iconic Reichstag, seat of the German parliament (Bundestag). Nearby, the Brandenburg Gate gives way to Unter den Linden, Berlin's most elegant boulevard, which flaunts its Prussian pedigree with pride.

Book an early time slot for the lift ride to the Reichstag (p40) dome and get the lay of the land while meandering up its spiralling ramp. Snap a picture of the Brandenburg Gate (p42), then get lost in the maze of the Holocaust Memorial (p44) before strolling over to architecturally stunning Gendarmenmarkt (p48). Enjoy a wiener schnitzel lunch at venerable Borchardt (p50), pick up a treat at Rausch Schokoladenhaus (p55) and spend a couple of hours delving into German history at the Deutsches Historisches Museum (p48). Indulge in a vegetarian dinner at Michelin-starred Cookies Cream (p50) before wrapping up the night with cocktails at chic Bar Tausend (p53).

Getting There & Around

🚌 Routes 100, 200 and TXL run along most of Unter den Linden.

S S1 and S2/25 stop at Brandenburger Tor and Friedrichstrasse.

U Stadtmitte (U2, U6), Französische Strasse (U6) and Hausvogteiplatz (U2) are all convenient stops for Gendarmenmarkt. For Unter den Linden, get off at Brandenburger Tor (U55), Friedrichstrasse (U6) or Französische Strasse (U6).

Reichstag & Unter Den Linden Map on p46

Deutsches Historisches Museum (p48) ANTONSHUTTERSTOCK/SHUTTERSTOCK ©

Top Sight
Reichstag & Government Quarter

The nexus of German political power snuggles neatly into the Spreebogen, a horseshoe-shaped bend in the Spree River. The historic anchor of the federal government quarter is the glass-domed Reichstag, which once rubbed against the western side of the Berlin Wall. It now forms part of a row of modern glass-and-concrete government buildings that symbolically link the former East and West Berlin across the Spree. North of the river looms the solar-panelled Hauptbahnhof (central train station).

⊙ MAP P46, C2

Platz der Republik 1

admission free

⏱ lift 8am-midnight, last entry 9.45pm, Visitors' Centre 8am-8pm Apr-Oct, to 6pm Nov-Mar

Ⓢ Brandenburger Tor, Hauptbahnhof, Ⓤ Brandenburger Tor, Bundestag

Reichstag Building

The four corner towers and mighty facade with the bronze dedication 'Dem Deutschen Volke' (To the German People; added in 1916) are the only original sections of the 1894 Reichstag. Norman Foster, the architectural mastermind of the building's post-reunification makeover, preserved only the historical shell and added the sparkling glass dome. The original dome, made of steel and glass and considered a high-tech marvel at the time, was destroyed during the Reichstag fire in 1933.

Reichstag Dome

Whoever said the best things in life are free might have been thinking of the lift ride up to the rooftop of the Reichstag. Enjoy the knock-out views, then pick up a free auto-activated audioguide and learn about the building, Berlin landmarks and the workings of the Bundestag while following the ramp spiralling up and around the dome's mirror-clad funnel.

Bundeskanzleramt

The Federal Chancellery, Germany's 'White House', is a sparkling, modern compound designed by Axel Schultes and Charlotte Frank and consists of two parallel office blocks flanking a central white cube. Eduardo Chillida's rusted-steel *Berlin* sculpture graces the forecourt.

Paul-Löbe-Haus

The glass-and-concrete Paul-Löbe-Haus houses offices for the Bundestag's parliamentary committees. A double footbridge links it to the Marie-Elisabeth-Lüders-Haus across the Spree in a visual symbol of reunification.

Marie-Elisabeth-Lüders-Haus

Home to the parliamentary library, this extravagant structure has a massive tapered stairway, a jutting roofline and giant circular windows. In the basement is an **art installation** by Ben Wagin featuring segments of the Berlin Wall.

★ Top Tips

o Advance reservations for visiting the Reichstag dome must be made online at www.bundestag.de.

o Without reservations, swing by the Reichstag Visitors' Centre in a nearby kiosk on Scheidemannstrasse to enquire about last-minute openings.

o Free multilingual guides are available on the roof terrace.

✕ Take a Break

o Book at least two weeks ahead for a table at the Dachgartenrestaurant Käfer (p52) on the Reichstag rooftop.

o For snacks and beer, report to the self-service **Berlin Pavillon** (☏030-2065 4737; www.berlin-pavillon.de; Scheidemannstrasse 1; dishes €4.50-9; ⊙8am-9pm; ☐100, ⑤Brandenburger Tor, ⑪Brandenburger Tor, Bundestag) on the edge of Tiergarten park.

Reichstag & Unter Den Linden Reichstag & Government Quarter

Top Sight 📷
Brandenburger Tor

The Brandenburg Gate is Berlin's most famous – and most photographed – landmark. Trapped right behind the Berlin Wall during the Cold War, it went from symbol of division to epitomising German reunification when the hated barrier fell in 1989. It now serves as a photogenic backdrop for raucous New Years' Eve parties, concerts, festivals and mega-events including FIFA World Cup finals.

◎ **MAP P46, D3**

Brandenburg Gate

Pariser Platz

S Brandenburger Tor,
U Brandenburger Tor

Origins

Commissioned by Prussian king Friedrich Wilhelm II, the gate was completed in 1791 as a symbol of peace and a suitably impressive entrance to the grand boulevard Unter den Linden. Architect Carl Gotthard Langhans looked to the Acropolis in Athens for inspiration for this elegant triumphal arch, which is the only surviving one of 18 city gates that once ringed historic Berlin.

Architecture

Standing 26m high, 65.5m wide and 11m deep, the neoclassical sandstone gate is fronted by 12 Doric columns and divided into five passageways. The wider central passage was reserved for the king and his entourage; common folk had to use the four narrower ones.

Quadriga

Crowning the Brandenburg Gate is the *Quadriga,* Johann Gottfried Schadow's famous sculpture of a winged goddess piloting a chariot drawn by four horses. After trouncing Prussia in 1806, Napoleon kidnapped the lady and held her hostage in Paris until a gallant Prussian general freed her in 1815. Afterwards, the goddess was equipped with a triumphal iron cross wrapped in an oak wreath and topped with a Prussian eagle.

Pariser Platz

Completely flattened in WWII, this once elegant square spent the Cold War trapped just east of the Berlin Wall. Look around now: the US, French and British embassies, banks and a luxury hotel have returned to their original sites and once again frame the bustling plaza, just as they did during its 19th-century heyday.

★ Top Tips

o If you need a moment of peace and quiet, visit the *Raum der Stille* (Room of Silence) in the gate's northern wing.

o There is a tourist office in the southern wing.

o The gate is at its most photogenic early in the morning and at sunset.

✕ Take a Break

o The cafe Weinwirtschaft inside the **Akademie der Künste** (Academy of Arts; ☏ 030-200 571 000; www.adk.de; Pariser Platz 4; admission varies; ⊙ Bldg 10am-8pm, exhibits vary; Ⓢ Brandenburger Tor, Ⓤ Brandenburger Tor) serves refreshments and international dishes.

o For a stylish break, enjoy coffee or champagne next to the elephant fountain in the lobby of the venerable **Hotel Adlon** (☏ 030-226 10; www.kempinski.com; Unter den Linden 77, Pariser Platz; Ⓢ Brandenburger Tor, Ⓤ Brandenburger Tor).

Top Sight 📷
Holocaust Memorial

*The **Denkmal für die ermordeten Juden Europas** (Memorial to the Murdered Jews of Europe) was officially dedicated in 2005. Colloquially known as Holocaust Memorial, it's Germany's central memorial to the Nazi-planned genocide during the Third Reich. For the football-field-sized space, New York architect Peter Eisenman created 2711 sarcophagus-like concrete stelae (slabs) of equal size but various heights, rising in sombre silence from the undulating ground.*

◎ MAP P46, D4

Memorial to the Murdered Jews of Europe

www.stiftung-denkmal.de

Cora-Berliner-Strasse 1

audioguide €3

🕘 24hr

S Brandenburger Tor,
U Brandenburger Tor

Field of Stelae

You're free to access this massive concrete maze at any point and make your individual journey through it. At first it may seem austere, even sterile. But take time to feel the coolness of the stone and contemplate the interplay of light and shadow, then stumble aimlessly among the narrow passageways, and you'll soon connect with a metaphorical sense of disorientation, confusion and claustrophobia.

Ort der Information

For context, visit the subterranean Ort der Information, which movingly lifts the veil of anonymity from the six million Holocaust victims. A graphic timeline of Jewish persecution during the Third Reich is followed by a series of rooms documenting the fates of individuals and families. The most visceral is the darkened **Room of Names**, where the names and years of birth and death of Jewish victims are projected onto all four walls while a solemn voice reads their short biographies. Poignant and heart-wrenching, these exhibits will leave no one untouched. Not recommended for children under 14.

Gay Memorial

Europe's LGBTQ+ community suffered enormously under the Nazis, as is commemorated by this freestanding, 4m-high, off-kilter concrete cube designed by Michael Elmgreen and Ingar Dragset. A looped video plays through a warped, narrow window.

Roma & Sinti Memorial

This memorial by Dani Karavan commemorates the Sinti and Roma victims of the Holocaust and consists of a circular reflecting pool with a floating stone decorated daily with a fresh flower.

★ **Top Tips**

o For a more in-depth experience, rent an audioguide (€3).

o Free 90-minute guided tours run at 3pm on Saturday in English and at 3pm on Sunday in German.

o The memorial is at its moodiest (and most photogenic) when shadows are long, ie early morning or late in the day.

✕ **Take a Break**

o For vegan and vegetarian in a modern setting, head to **Samadhi** (☏030-2248 8850; www.samadhi-vegetarian.de; Wilhelmstrasse 77; mains €9-15; ⏰noon-11pm; 🛜🌱; 🚌200, Ⓢ Brandenburger Tor, Ⓤ Brandenburger Tor).

o Lots of eating and drinking options, including healthy dishes at Ki-Nova (p87), are a short stroll south at Potsdamer Platz.

Reichstag & Unter Den Linden

Alt-Moabit
Rahel-Hirsch-Str
Kapelleufer
Schumannstr
Moltkebrücke
SpreeRiver
Spreebogenpark
Karlplatz
Willy-Brandt-Str
Otto-von-Bismarck-Allee
Marie-Elisabeth-Lüders-Haus
Luisenstr
Bundestag
Bundeskanzleramt
Paul-Löbe-Haus
Paul-Löbe-Allee
Haus der Kulturen der Welt
Platz der Republik
Reichstag
Heinrich-von-Gagern-Str
Scheidemannstr
John-Foster-Dulles-Allee
Yitzhak-Rabin-Str
Ebertstr
Pariser Platz
Platz des 18 März
Brandenburger Tor
Strasse des 17 Juni
Brandenburger Tor
Holocaust Memorial
Tiergartentunnel
Tiergarten
Cora-Berliner-Str
Hannah-Arendt-Str
Site of Hitler's Bunker
Bellevueallee
In den Ministergärten
Gertrud-Kolmar-Str
Kemperplatz
Lennéstr
Am Park
Ebertstr
Vossstr
Tiergartenstr
Bellevuestr
Ben-Gurion-Str
Leipziger Platz
Potsdamer Str
Potsdamer Platz
Alte Potsdamer Str

For reviews see
- Top Sights — p40
- Sights — p48
- Eating — p50
- Drinking — p53
- Entertainment — p53
- Shopping — p55

E **F** **G** **H**

1

Reinhardtstr

Ziegelstr

Monbijou Park

Marienstr

Albrechtstr

Bertolt-Brecht-Platz

Spree River

Am Weidendamm

Monbijoustr

Geschwister-Scholl-Str

Johannisstr

MUSEUMSINSEL

16

Tränenpalast

3

Friedrichstr

Planckstr

Am Kupfergraben

Spreekanal

2

Schiffbauerdamm

Bahnhof Friedrichstr

Georgenstr

Bauhofstr

Bodestr

Reichstagufer

Friedrichstr

Dorotheenstr

Mittelstr

Charlottenstr

Universitätsstr

Am Zeughaus

Am Festungsgraben

5
Neue Wache

1
Deutsches Historisches Museum

Oberwallstr

3

7 *Madame Tussauds*

8 ✕

17 ☆

Schlossbrücke

Unter den Linden

18 ☆

15

Behrenstr

Behrenstr

20 ☆

Kurstr

Französische Str

10 ✕

Französische Str

11

Jägerstr

13 ✕

4

Wilhelmstr

Mauerstr

Glinkastr

24 🔒

Friedrichstr

Jägerstr

19 **2**
☆ *Gendarmenmarkt*

Taubenstr

Hausvogteiplatz 🚇

Hausvogteiplatz

12

Niederwallstr

Jerusalemer Str

Taubenstr

Hochschule für Musik Hanns Eisler

Mohrenstr

Mohrenstr 🚇

Mohrenstr

Stadtmitte 🚇

23

Kronenstr

5

Vossstr

Stadtmitte 🚇

Leipziger Str

Leipziger Str

Leipziger Str

Schützenstr

6

Zimmerstr

Friedrichstr

21 🔒

Zimmerstr

🧭 **N** 0 _____ 400 m
0 _____ 0.2 miles

E **F** **G** **H**

Sights

Deutsches Historisches Museum
MUSEUM

1 ⊙ MAP P46, H3

If you're wondering what the Germans have been up to for the past 1500 years, take a spin around the baroque Zeughaus, formerly the Prussian arsenal and now home of the German Historical Museum. Upstairs, displays concentrate on the period from the 6th century AD to the end of WWI in 1918, while the ground floor tracks the 20th century all the way through to the early years after German reunification. (German Historical Museum; ☏030-203 040; www.dhm.de; Unter den Linden 2; adult/concession/child under 18 incl IM Pei Bau €8/4/free; ⊙10am-6pm; ☐100, 200, Ⓤ Hausvogteiplatz, Ⓢ Hackescher Markt)

Gendarmenmarkt
SQUARE

2 ⊙ MAP P46, G4

This graceful square is bookended by the domed German and French cathedrals and punctuated by a grandly porticoed concert hall, the **Konzerthaus** (☏030-203 092 333; www.konzerthaus.de; Gendarmenmarkt 2; Ⓤ Französische Strasse, Stadtmitte). It was named for the Gens d'Armes, an 18th-century Prussian regiment consisting of French Huguenot refugees. (Ⓤ Französische Strasse, Stadtmitte)

Tränenpalast
MUSEUM

3 ⊙ MAP P46, F2

During the Cold War, tears flowed copiously in this glass-and-steel border-crossing pavilion where East Berliners had to bid adieu to family visiting from West Germany – hence its 'Palace of Tears' moniker. The exhibit uses original objects (including the claustrophobic passport control booths and a border auto-firing system), photographs and historical footage to document the division's social impact on the daily lives of Germans on both sides of the border. (☏030-4677 77911; www.hdg.de; Reichstagufer 17; admission free; ⊙9am-7pm Tue-Fri, 10am-6pm Sat & Sun; Ⓢ Friedrichstrasse, Ⓤ Friedrichstrasse)

Haus der Kulturen der Welt
NOTABLE BUILDING

4 ⊙ MAP P46, A2

This highly respected cultural centre showcases contemporary non-European art, music, dance, literature, films and theatre, and also serves as a discussion forum on zeitgeist-reflecting issues. The gravity-defying parabolic roof of Hugh Stubbins' extravagant building, designed as the American contribution to a 1957 architectural exhibition, is echoed by Henry Moore's sculpture *Butterfly* in the reflecting pool. (House of World Cultures; ☏030-3978 7175; www.hkw.de; John-Foster-Dulles-Allee 10; admission varies; ⊙exhibits 11am-7pm Wed-Mon; Ⓟ; ☐100, Ⓢ Hauptbahnhof, Ⓤ Bundestag, Hauptbahnhof)

Neue Wache

MEMORIAL

5 ⊙ MAP P46, H3

This temple-like neoclassical structure (1818) was Karl Friedrich Schinkel's first important Berlin commission. Originally a royal guardhouse and a memorial to the victims of the Napoleonic Wars, it is now Germany's central memorial for the victims of war and dictatorship. Its sombre and austere interior is dominated by Käthe Kollwitz' heart-wrenching Pietà-style sculpture of a mother helplessly cradling her dead soldier son. (New Guardhouse; Unter den Linden 4; admission free; ⊙10am-6pm; 🚌100, 200, TXL)

Site of Hitler's Bunker

HISTORIC SITE

6 ⊙ MAP P46, D4

Berlin was burning and Soviet tanks advancing relentlessly when Adolf Hitler killed himself on 30 April 1945, alongside Eva Braun, his long-time female companion, hours after their marriage. Today, a parking lot covers the site, revealing its dark history only via an information panel with a diagram of the vast bunker network, construction data and the site's post-WWII history. (cnr In den Ministergärten & Gertrud-Kolmar-Strasse; ⊙24hr; 🅂Brandenburger Tor, 🅄Brandenburger Tor)

Konzerthaus Berlin (p54) looms over Gendarmenmarkt (p48)

Madame Tussauds   MUSEUM

7 MAP P46, E3

No celebrity in town to snare your stare? Don't fret: at this legendary wax museum, the world's biggest pop stars, Hollywood legends, sports heroes and historical icons stand still – very still – for you to snap their picture. Sure, it's an expensive haven of kitsch and camp, but where else can you have a candlelit dinner with George Clooney, play piano with Beethoven or time-travel to the '70s with Ziggy Stardust? Avoid queues and save money by buying tickets online. (☎01806-545 800; www.madametus sauds.com/berlin; Unter den Linden 74; adult/child €23.50/18.50; ⏲10am-6pm Mon-Fri, to 7pm Sat & Sun, last entry 1hr before closing; ☒100, ⑤Branden-burger Tor, ⓊBrandenburger Tor)

Eating

Cookies Cream   VEGETARIAN €€€

8 ✖ MAP P46, F3

In 2017, this perennial local favourite became Berlin's first flesh-free restaurant to enter the Michelin pantheon, on its 10th anniversary no less. Its industrial look and clandestine location are as unorthodox as the compositions of head chef Stephan Hentschel. The entrance is off the service alley of the Westin Grand Hotel (past the chandelier, ring the bell). (☎030-2749 2940; www.cookiescream.com; Behrenstrasse 55; mains €25, 3-/4-course menu €49/59; ⏲6pm-midnight Tue-Sat; ✎; ⓊFranzösische Strasse)

India Club   NORTH INDIAN €€

9 ✖ MAP P46, D4

No need to book a flight to Mumbai or London: authentic Indian cuisine has finally landed in Berlin. Thanks to top toque Manish Bahukhandi, these curries are like culinary poetry, the chicken tikka perfectly succulent and the stuffed cauliflower an inspiration. The dark mahogany furniture is enlivened by splashes of colour in the plates, the chandeliers and the servers' uniforms. (☎030-2062 8610; www.india-club-berlin.com; Behrenstrasse 72; mains €16-27; ⏲6-10.30pm; ✎; ⑤Brandenburger Tor)

Borchardt   FRENCH €€€

10 ✖ MAP P46, F4

Jagger, Clooney and Redford are among the celebs who have tucked into dry-aged steaks and plump oysters in the marble-pillared dining hall of this Berlin institution, established in 1853 by a caterer to the Kaiser. No dish, however, moves as fast as the Wiener Schnitzel, a wafer-thin slice of breaded veal fried to crisp perfection. (☎030-8188 6262; www.borchardt-restaurant.de; Französische Strasse 47; dinner mains €20-40; ⏲11.30am-midnight; ⓊFranzösische Strasse)

Augustiner am Gendarmenmarkt   GERMAN €€

11 ✖ MAP P46, G4

Tourists, concertgoers and hearty-food lovers rub shoulders at rustic tables in this authentic Bavarian

Berlin under the Swastika

The rise to power of Adolf Hitler and the NSDAP (Nazi Party) in January 1933 had instant and far-reaching consequences for all of Germany. Within three months, all non-Nazi parties, organisations and labour unions had been outlawed and many political opponents, intellectuals and artists detained without trial. Jews, of course, were a main target from the start but the horror escalated for them during the Kristallnacht pogroms on 9 November 1938, when Nazi thugs desecrated, burned and demolished synagogues and Jewish cemeteries, property and businesses across the country. Jews had begun to emigrate after 1933, but this event set off a stampede.

The fate of those Jews who stayed behind is well known: their systematic, bureaucratic and meticulously documented annihilation in death camps, mostly in Nazi-occupied territories in Eastern Europe. Sinti and Roma (gypsies), political opponents, priests, gays, the disabled and habitual criminals were targeted as well. Of the roughly seven million people who were sent to concentration camps, only 500,000 survived.

The Battle of Berlin

With the Normandy invasion of June 1944, Allied troops arrived in formidable force on the European mainland, supported by unrelenting air raids on Berlin and most other German cities. The final Battle of Berlin began in mid-April 1945, with 1.5 million Soviet troops barrelling towards the city from the east. On 30 April, when the fighting reached the government quarter, Hitler and his long-time companion Eva Braun killed themselves in their bunker. As their bodies were burning, Red Army soldiers raised the Soviet flag above the Reichstag.

Defeat & Aftermath

The Battle of Berlin ended on 2 May, with Germany's unconditional surrender six days later. The fighting had taken an enormous toll on Berlin and its people. Much of the city lay in smouldering rubble and at least 125,000 Berliners had lost their lives. In July 1945, the leaders of the Allies met in Potsdam to carve up Germany and Berlin into four zones of occupation controlled by Britain, the USA, the USSR and France.

beer hall. Soak up the down-to-earth vibe right along with a mug of full-bodied Augustiner brew

straight from Munich. Sausages, roast pork and pretzels provide rib-sticking sustenance with only a token salad offered for non-carnivores. Good-value weekday lunch specials. (☎030-2045 4020; www.augustiner-braeu-berlin.de; Charlottenstrasse 55; mains €7.50-30, lunch special €5.90; ⏰10am-2am; Ⓤ Französische Strasse)

Goodtime
THAI €€

13 Ⓧ MAP P46, H4

Sweep on down to this busy dining room with a garden courtyard for fragrant Thai and Indonesian dishes. Creamy curries, succulent shrimp or roast duck all taste flavourful and fresh, if a bit easy on the heat to accommodate German stomachs. If you like it hot, order Api Sapi (aka 'beef in hell'). (☎030-2007 4870; www.goodtime-berlin.de; Hausvogteiplatz 11; mains

---

€12.50-25; ⏰noon-midnight; 🍴; Ⓤ Hausvogteiplatz)

Chipps
VEGETARIAN €

13 Ⓧ MAP P46, H4

This crisp corner spot with a show-kitchen and panoramic windows is a great day-time destination, which turns heads with yummy cooked breakfasts (served any time), build-your-own salads and creative hot specials that spin regional, seasonal ingredients into taste-bud magic. Dinners are more elaborate. (☎030-3644 4588; www.chipps.eu; Jägerstrasse 35; mains breakfast €7.50-11.50, salads €7.50-12.50; ⏰9am-11pm Mon-Sat, to 5pm Sun; 🛜🍴; Ⓤ Hausvogteiplatz)

Dachgartenrestaurant Käfer im Bundestag
INTERNATIONAL €€€

14 Ⓧ MAP P46, C2

While politicians debate treaties and taxes in the plenary hall below, you can enjoy breakfast and hot meals with a regional bent at the restaurant on the Reichstag rooftop. Reservations here also give you direct access to the landmark glass dome crowning the building; book at least two weeks ahead.

Note that for security reasons, all guests must provide their name and date of birth at least 24 hours in advance. (☎030-226 2990; www.feinkost-kaefer.de/berlin; Platz der Republik; mains €24-33; ⏰9am-4.30pm & 6.30pm-midnight; 🚌100, Ⓤ Bundestag)

Rebuilt Glamour Pad: Hotel Adlon

On Pariser Platz, overlooking the Brandenburg Gate, the **Hotel Adlon** is one of Berlin's poshest and most storied hotels. In 1932 the movie *Grand Hotel* starring Greta Garbo was partly filmed here. Destroyed in WWII and rebuilt in the 1990s, today's edition is a near-replica of the 1907 original and remains a favourite haunt of celebs, politicians and the merely moneyed. Remember Michael Jackson dangling his baby out of the window? It happened at the Adlon.

TONO BALAGUER/SHUTTERSTOCK ©

Staatsoper Berlin

Drinking

Rooftop Terrace
BAR

15 🚇 MAP P46, G3

A refined ambience reigns at the rooftop bar of the exclusive **Hotel de Rome** (📞030-460 6090; www.roccofortehotels.com; Behrenstrasse 37; 🚌100, 200, TXL, 🚇Hausvogteiplatz), where you can keep an eye on the Fernsehturm (TV Tower), historic landmarks and the construction projects along Unter den Linden. It's a chill spot for an afternoon coffee, a glass of homemade ginger lemonade or sunset cocktails with bar snacks. (📞030-460 6090; www.roccofortehotels.com; Behrenstrasse 37, Hotel de Rome; ⏰3-11pm Mon-Fri, from noon Sat & Sun May-Sep, weather permitting; 🛜; 🚌100, 200, TXL, 🚇Hausvogteiplatz)

Bar Tausend
BAR

16 🚇 MAP P46, E2

No sign, no light, no bell; just an anonymous steel door tucked under a railway bridge leads to one of Berlin's chicest clandestine bars. The tunnel-shaped space is clad in mirrors and bookended by a dance floor and a giant light fixture resembling an eye. DJs and bands fuel the glam vibe nightly. Selective door. (www.tausendberlin.com; Schiffbauerdamm 11; ⏰7.30pm-late Tue-Sat; 🚇Friedrichstrasse, 🚇Friedrichstrasse)

Entertainment

Staatsoper Berlin
OPERA

17 ⭐ MAP P46, G3

After a seven-year exile, Berlin's most famous opera company once again performs at the venerable

Free Concerts in Royal Stables

The gifted students at Berlin's top-rated classical music academy, the **Hochschule für Musik Hanns Eisler** (Map p46, G4; ☑ tickets 030-203 092 101; www.hfm-berlin.de; Charlottenstrasse 55; Ⓤ Stadtmitte, Französische Strasse), showcase their talents at up to 400 performances annually, many of them in the **Neuer Marstall** (Schlossplatz 7), where the Prussian royals once kept their coaches and horses. Many concerts are free or low-cost. See the website for the full schedule.

neoclassical Staatsoper Unter den Linden, which emerged from a massive refurbishment in 2017. Its repertory includes works from four centuries along with concerts and classical and modern ballet, all under the musical leadership of Daniel Barenboim. (☑ 030-2035 4554; www.staatsoper-berlin.de; Unter den Linden 7; tickets €12-250; 🚌 100, 200, TXL, Ⓤ Französische Strasse)

Komische Oper
OPERA

18 ⭐ MAP P46, F3

The smallest among Berlin's trio of opera houses is also its least stuffy, even if its flashy neo-baroque auditorium might suggest otherwise. Productions are innovative and unconventional – yet top quality – and often reinterpret classic (and sometimes obscure) pieces in zeitgeist-capturing ways. Seats feature an ingenious subtitling system in English, Turkish and other languages. (Comic Opera; ☑ tickets 030-4799 7400; www.komische-oper-berlin.de; Behrenstrasse 55-57; tickets €12-90; ⏰ box office 11am-7pm Mon-Sat, 1-4pm Sun; 🚌 100, 200, TXL, Ⓤ Französische Strasse)

Konzerthaus Berlin
CLASSICAL MUSIC

19 ⭐ MAP P46, G4

This lovely classical music venue – a Schinkel design from 1821 – counts the top-ranked Konzerthausorchester Berlin as its 'house band', but also hosts visiting soloists and orchestras in three venues. For a sightseeing break, check the schedule for weekly one-hour lunchtime 'Espresso Concerts' costing a mere €8. (☑ tickets 030-203 092 101; www.konzerthaus. de; Gendarmenmarkt 2; tickets €15-85; Ⓤ Stadtmitte, Französische Strasse)

Pierre Boulez Saal
CONCERT VENUE

20 ⭐ MAP P46, H4

Open since 2017, this intimate concert hall was designed by Frank Gehry and conceived by Daniel Barenboim as a venue to promote dialogue between cultures through music. The musical line-up spans the arc from classical to jazz, electronic to Arab music, performed by top-flight international artists, students of the affiliated Barenboim-Said Academy as well as the Boulez

Ensemble. (☎tickets 030-4799 7411; www.boulezsaal.de; Französische Strasse 33d; tickets €10-65; 🚌100, 200, TXL, 147, ⓊHausvogteiplatz, Stadtmitte)

Shopping

Frau Tonis Parfum   PERFUME

21 🅰 MAP P46, F6

Follow your nose to this scent-sational made-in-Berlin perfume boutique, where a 'scent test' reveals if you're the floral, fruity, woody or oriental type to help you choose a matching fragrance. Bestsellers include the fresh and light 'Berlin Summer'. Individualists can have their own customised blend created in a one-hour session (€125, including 50ml eau de parfum; reservations advised). (☎030-2021 5310; www.frau-tonis-parfum.com; Zimmerstrasse 13; ⏱10am-6pm Mon-Sat; ⓊKochstrasse)

Dussmann – Das Kulturkaufhaus   BOOKS

22 🅰 MAP P46, F3

It's easy to lose track of time in this cultural playground with wall-to-wall books (including an extensive English section), DVDs and CDs, leaving no genre unaccounted for. Bonus points for the downstairs cafe, the vertical garden, and the performance space used for free concerts, political discussions and high-profile book readings and signings. (☎030-2025 1111; www.kulturkaufhaus.de;

Friedrichstrasse 90; ⏱9am-11.30pm Mon-Sat; 📶; Ⓢ Friedrichstrasse, ⓊFriedrichstrasse)

Rausch Schokoladenhaus   CHOCOLATE

23 🅰 MAP P46, G5

If the Aztecs regarded chocolate as the elixir of the gods, then this emporium of truffles and pralines must be heaven. The shop features Insta-worthy replicas of Berlin landmarks such as the Brandenburg Gate and Fernsehturm (TV Tower), while the upstairs cafe-restaurant delivers views of Gendarmenmarkt along with sinful drinking chocolates and artsy handmade cakes and *tartes*. (☎030-757 880; www.rausch.de; Charlottenstrasse 60; ⏱10am-8pm Mon-Sat, from 11am Sun; ⓊStadtmitte)

Galeries Lafayette   DEPARTMENT STORE

24 🅰 MAP P46, F4

Stop by the Berlin branch of the exquisite French fashion emporium if only to check out the show-stealing interior (designed by Jean Nouvel, no less), centred on a huge glass cone shimmering with kaleidoscopic intensity. Around it wrap three circular floors filled with fancy fashions, fragrances and accessories, while glorious gourmet treats await in the basement food hall. (☎030-209 480; www.galerieslafayette.de; Friedrichstrasse 76-78; ⏱10am-8pm Mon-Sat; ⓊFranzösische Strasse)

Explore ◈
Museum Island & Alexanderplatz

Sightseers hit the jackpot in this historic area, headlined by Museum Island, a Unesco-recognised cluster of five world-class repositories brimming with six millennia of artistic expression. The Berliner Dom watches serenely over it all, including the Humboldt Forum, a soon-to-open cultural centre in a reconstructed royal palace. For an even grander perspective, ride up the TV Tower, Germany's highest structure.

Beat the crowds by heading to Museum Island first thing to marvel at ancient treasures in the Pergamon-museum (p58) and the Neues Museum (p62). Relax over refreshments in the latter's café or peruse the panorama of Berliner Dom (p66), Altes Museum (p66) and Humboldt Forum (p69) while chilling on the Lustgarten lawn. Travel behind the Iron Curtain at the playful DDR Museum (p65), then process your impressions on a boat ride through the historic centre. Beer o'clock! Head to Strandbar Mitte (p71). Stay for pizza and dancing or indulge in a traditional German meal at Brauhaus Georgbräu (p68).

Getting There & Around

🚌 M48 and 200 link Alexanderplatz with Potsdamer Platz; bus 247 goes to the Nikolaiviertel.

Ⓢ S5, S7 and S75 all converge at Alexanderplatz.

Ⓤ U2, U5 and U8 stop at Alexanderplatz. Other main stops are Klosterstrasse and Märkisches Museum (U2) and Jannowitzbrücke (U8).

Museum Island & Alexanderplatz Map on p64

Fernsehturm (p65), Alexanderplatz CANADASTOCK/SHUTTERSTOCK ©

Top Sight 📷

Pergamonmuseum

Even while undergoing gradual renovation, the Pergamonmuseum opens a fascinating window onto the ancient world. The palatial three-wing complex presents a feast of classical sculpture and architecture from Greece, Rome, Babylon and the Middle East. Most of the pieces were excavated and spirited to Berlin by German archaeologists around the turn of the 20th century. Note that the north wing and the hall containing the namesake Pergamon Altar will be closed until 2023.

◉ MAP P64, B2

www.smb.museum

Bodestrasse 1-3

adult/concession/under 18yr €12/6/free

🕙 10am-6pm Fri-Wed, to 8pm Thu

Ⓢ Hackescher Markt, Friedrichstrasse, Ⓤ Friedrichstrasse

Market Gate of Miletus

Merchants and customers once flooded through this splendid 17m-high gate into the bustling market square of Miletus, a wealthy Roman trading town in present-day Turkey. A strong earthquake levelled much of the town in the early Middle Ages, but German archaeologists dug up the site between 1903 and 1905 and managed to put the puzzle back together. The richly decorated marble gate blends Greek and Roman design features and is the world's single largest monument ever to be reassembled in a museum.

Ishtar Gate

Step through the Gate of Miletus and travel back 800 years to yet another culture and civilisation: Babylon during the reign of King Nebuchadnezzar II (604–562 BC).It's impossible not to be awed by the magnificence of the **Ishtar Gate** (pictured left), the **Processional Way** leading to it and the facade of the **king's throne hall**. All are sheathed in radiant blue glazed bricks and adorned with ochre reliefs of strutting lions, bulls and dragons representing Babylonian gods. They're so striking, you can almost hear the roaring and fanfare as the procession rolls into town.

Clay Tablets from Uruk

Founded in the 4th millennium BC, Uruk (in present-day Iraq) is considered one of the world's first 'mega-cities', with as many as 40,000 inhabitants and more than 9km of city walls. Among the museum's most prized possessions are clay tablets with cuneiform scripts detailing agreements and transactions that are considered the earliest written documents known to humankind.

★ Top Tips

o During the revamp, the museum entrance is off Bodestrasse, behind the Neues Museum.

o Admission is free for those under 18.

o Arrive early or late on weekdays, or skip the queues by purchasing your ticket online.

o Make use of the excellent multilanguage audioguides included in the admission price.

✗ Take a Break

o Combat sightseeing fatigue at a riverside terrace table with terrific views of the Berliner Dom at the modern **Allegretto Gran Cafe** (☎030-308 777 517; Anna-Louisa-Karsch-Strasse 2; mains €10-13; ◷10am-8pm; 🛜; 🚌100, 200, TXL, SHackescher Markt).

o In summer, head to Strandbar Mitte (p71) for alfresco refreshments and pizza with a view of Museumsinsel across the Spree River.

Statue of Hadad

A vast room crammed with treasures from ancient Assyria is lorded over by a monumental 2800-year-old statue of a fierce-looking Hadad, the West Semitic god of storm, thunder and rain. Also note the four lion sculptures guarding the partly reconstructed inner gate of the citadel of Samal (in today's Turkey).

Caliph's Palace of Mshatta

When Ottoman Sultan Abdul Hamid II wanted to get into German Emperor Wilhelm II's good graces, he him a most generous gift; the facade of the 8th-century palace of Mshatta, in today's Jordan. A masterpiece of early Islamic art, it depicts animals and mythical creatures frolicking peacefully amid a riot of floral motifs in an allusion to the Garden of Eden.

Aleppo Room

Guests arriving at this richly painted, wood-panelled reception room would have had no doubt as to the wealth and power of its owner, a Christian merchant in 17th-century Aleppo, Syria. The beautiful, if dizzying, paintings depict both Christian themes and courtly scenes like those portrayed in Persian book illustrations, suggesting a high level of religious tolerance. Look closely to make out the Last Supper to the right of the central door.

Alhambra Domed Roof

A domed cedar and poplar ceiling from the Torre de las Damas (Ladies' Tower) of the Alhambra in southern

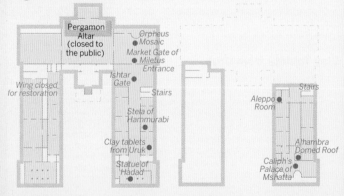

Pergamonmuseum

Ground Floor

- Pergamon Altar (closed to the public)
- Wing closed for restoration
- Orpheus Mosaic
- Market Gate of Miletus
- Entrance
- Ishtar Gate
- Stairs
- Stela of Hammurabi
- Clay tablets from Uruk
- Statue of Hadad

Upper Floor

- Stairs
- Aleppo Room
- Alhambra Domed Roof
- Caliph's Palace of Mshatta

Museum Island Masterplan

The Pergamonmuseum is part of Museum Island (Museumsinsel), a cluster of five museums built between 1830 and 1930 and declared a Unesco World Heritage Site in 1999. The distinction was at least partly achieved because of a master plan for the renovation and modernisation of the complex, which is expected to be completed in 2026 under the aegis of British architect David Chipperfield. Except for the Pergamon, now under partial renovation, the restoration of the buildings has been completed. Construction is also well under way on the colonnaded **James-Simon-Galerie**. Expected to open in 2019, it will serve as the central visitors centre and provide direct access to the Pergamonmuseum and the Neues Museum. It will also lead to the 'Archaeological Promenade', a subterranean walkway set to link the Altes Museum with the Bode-Museum in the north. For full details see www.museumsinsel-berlin.de.

Spain's Granada forms the 'lid of the Moorish Cabinet' upstairs. Intricately patterned, it centres on a 16-pointed star from which radiate 16 triangular panels inlaid with decorative elements.

Asisi Panorama

While the Pergamon Altar is being restored, visitors can grasp its impressive beauty in a temporary exhibit in a purpose-built rotunda off the northern tip of Museum Island. Against the backdrop of a monumental 360° panorama of the city in AD 129, created by Yadegar Asisi, it displays 80 original sculptures from the excavation site, including a colossal head of Heracles and a section from the famous Telephos frieze.

Top Sight 📷
Neues Museum

David Chipperfield's reconstruction of the bombed-out Neues Museum (New Museum) on Museum Island is the residence of Queen Nefertiti, the showstopper of the Ägyptisches Museum (Egyptian Museum) alongside the enthralling Museum für Vor- und Frühgeschichte (Museum of Pre- and Early History). The British architect incorporated every original shard, scrap and brick he could find into the new building, creating a dynamic blend of the historic and the modern.

◎ MAP P64, B3

www.smb.museum

Bodestrasse 1-3

adult/concession/under 18yr €12/6/free

🕙 10am-6pm Fri-Wed, to 8pm Thu

S Hackescher Markt, Friedrichstrasse,

U Friedrichstrasse

Nefertiti

An audience with Berlin's most beautiful woman, the 3300-year-old Egyptian Queen Nefertiti – she of the long graceful neck and eternally good looks – is a must. Extremely well preserved, the sculpture was part of the treasure trove unearthed around 1912 by a Berlin expedition of archaeologists who were sifting through the sands of Armana, the royal city built by Nefertiti's husband, King Akhenaten.

Berliner Goldhut

Resembling a wizard's hat, the 3000-year-old Berlin Gold Hat must indeed have struck the Bronze Age people as something magical. The entire cone is swathed in elaborate bands of astrological symbols believed to have helped priests calculate the movements of sun and moon and thus predict the best times for planting and harvesting. It's one of only four unearthed worldwide.

Berlin Grüner Kopf

Another famous work is the so-called Berlin Green Head – the bald head of a priest carved from smooth green stone. Created around 400 BC in the Late Egyptian Period, it shows Greek influence and is unusual in that it is not an actual portrait of a specific person but an idealised figure meant to exude universal wisdom and experience.

Trojan Collection

In 1870 German archaeologist Heinrich Schliemann discovered a stunning hoard of treasures from ancient Troy while digging around near Hisarlik in modern-day Turkey. Alas, most of the elaborate jewellery, ornate weapons and gold mugs on display are replicas because the originals became Soviet war booty after WWII and remain in Moscow.

★ Top Tips

o Skip the queue by buying advance tickets online.

o If you plan on visiting more than one museum on Museum Island, save money by buying the Museumsinsel ticket (€18, concession €9), good for one-day admission to all five museums.

o Admission is free for those under 18.

✕ Take a Break

Allegretto (☎030-2804 2307; www.allegretto-neuesmuseum.de; Neues Museum, Bodestrasse 1; dishes €3-10; ☉10am-6pm Fri-Wed, to 8pm Thu; ⛙100, 200, TXL, ⓢHackescher Markt), the lovely cafe inside the Neues Museum serves sandwiches, salads, Arabic dishes and wonderful cakes baked in-house.

Museum Island & Alexanderplatz

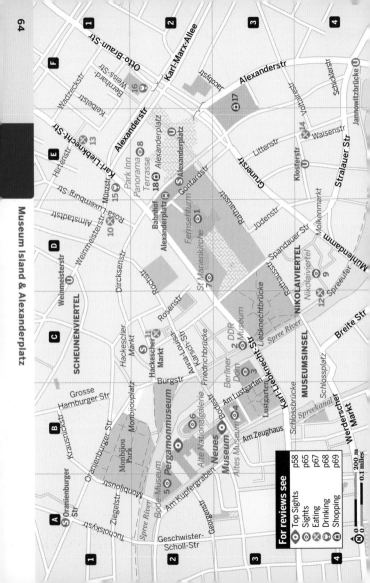

200 m
0.1 miles

Sights

Fernsehturm

LANDMARK

1 ◉ MAP P64, D2

Germany's tallest structure, the TV Tower has been soaring 368m high since 1969 and is as iconic to Berlin as the Eiffel Tower is to Paris. On clear days, views are stunning from the observation deck (with bar) at 203m or from the upstairs **Sphere restaurant** (207m), which makes one revolution per hour. (TV Tower; ☎030-247 575 875; www.tv-turm.de; Panoramastrasse 1a; adult/child €15.50/9.50, fast track online ticket €19.50/12; ⊙9am-midnight Mar-Oct, 10am-midnight Nov-Feb, last ascent 11.30pm; 🚌100, 200, TXL, Ⓤ Alexanderplatz, Ⓢ Alexanderplatz)

DDR Museum

MUSEUM

2 ◉ MAP P64, C3

This touchy-feely museum does an insightful and entertaining job of pulling back the iron curtain on daily life in socialist East Germany. You'll learn how kids were put through collective potty training, engineers earned little more than farmers, and everyone, it seems, went on nudist holidays. A perennial crowd-pleaser among the historic objects on display is a Trabi, the tinny East German standard car – sit in it to take a virtual spin around an East Berlin neighbourhood. (GDR (East Germany) Museum; ☎030-847 123 731; www.ddr-museum.de; Karl-Liebknecht-Strasse 1; adult/concession €9.80/6; ⊙10am-8pm Sun-Fri, to 10pm Sat; 🚌100, 200, TXL, Ⓢ Hackescher Markt)

DDR Museum

Berliner Dom CHURCH

3 ⊙ MAP P64, C3

Pompous yet majestic, the Italian Renaissance–style former royal court church (1905) does triple duty as house of worship, museum and concert hall. Inside it's gilt to the hilt and outfitted with a lavish marble-and-onyx altar, a 7269-pipe Sauer organ and elaborate royal sarcophagi. Climb up the 267 steps to the gallery for glorious city views. (Berlin Cathedral; 📞 box office 030-2026 9136; www.berlinerdom.de; Am Lustgarten; adult/concession €7/5; ⊙9am-8pm Apr-Sep, to 7pm Oct-Mar; 🚌100, 200, TXL, Ⓢ Hackescher Markt)

Altes Museum MUSEUM

4 ⊙ MAP P64, B3

A curtain of fluted columns gives way to the Pantheon-inspired rotunda of the grand neoclassical Old Museum, which harbours a prized antiquities collection. In the downstairs galleries, sculptures, vases, tomb reliefs and jewellery shed light on various facets of life in ancient Greece, while upstairs the focus is on the Etruscans and Romans. Top draws include the *Praying Boy* bronze sculpture, Roman silver vessels, an 'erotic cabinet' (over 18s only!) and portraits of Caesar and Cleopatra. (Old Museum; 📞030-266 424 242; www.smb.museum; Am Lustgarten; adult/concession/under 18 €10/5/free; ⊙10am-6pm Tue, Wed & Fri-Sun, to 8pm Thu; 🚌100, 200, TXL, Ⓢ Friedrichstrasse, Hackescher Markt, Ⓤ Friedrichstrasse)

Bode-Museum MUSEUM

5 ⊙ MAP P64, A2

On the northern tip of Museumsinsel, this palatial edifice houses a comprehensive collection of European sculpture from the early Middle Ages to the 18th century, including priceless masterpieces by Tilman Riemenschneider, Donatello and Giovanni Pisano. Other rooms harbour a precious coin collection and a smattering of Byzantine art, including sarcophagi and ivory carvings. (📞030-266 424 242; www.smb.museum; cnr Am Kupfergraben & Monbijoubrücke; adult/concession/under 18 €12/6/free; ⊙10am-6pm Tue, Wed & Fri-Sun, to 8pm Thu; Ⓢ Hackescher Markt, Friedrichstrasse)

Alte Nationalgalerie MUSEUM

6 ⊙ MAP P64, B2

The Greek temple–style Old National Gallery is a three-storey showcase of 19th-century European art. To get a sense of the period's virtuosity, pay special attention to the moody landscapes by Romantic heart-throb Caspar David Friedrich, the epic canvases by Franz Krüger and Adolf Menzel glorifying Prussia, the Gothic fantasies of Karl Friedrich Schinkel, and the sprinkling of French and German impressionists. (Old National Gallery; 📞030-266 424 242; www.smb.museum; Bodestrasse 1-3; adult/concession €10/5; ⊙10am-6pm Tue, Wed & Fri-Sun, to 8pm Thu; 🚌100, 200, TXL, Ⓢ Hackescher Markt)

Eating

St Marienkirche CHURCH

7 MAP P64, D2

This Gothic gem has welcomed worshippers since the early 14th century, making it one of Berlin's oldest surviving churches. A 22m-long *Dance of Death* fresco in the vestibule inspired by a 15th-century plague leads to a relatively plain interior enlivened by numerous other art treasures. The oldest is the 1437 bronze baptismal font buttressed by a trio of dragons. The baroque alabaster pulpit by Andreas Schlüter from 1703 is equally eye-catching. (St Mary's Church; www.marienkirche-berlin.de; Karl-Liebknecht-Strasse 8; ⏰10am-6pm Apr-Dec, to 4pm Jan-Mar; 🚌100, 200, TXL, 🚇Hackescher Markt, Alexanderplatz, Ⓤ Alexanderplatz)

Park Inn Panorama Terrasse VIEWPOINT

8 MAP P64, E2

For city views at eye level with the Fernsehturm (TV Tower), head up to the rooftop Panorama Terrasse, the open-air lounge of the Park Inn Hotel, some 150m above Alexanderplatz. Grab a sunlounger and relax with a cold beer or a glass of bubbly. (☎030-238 90; www.parkinn-berlin.de/en/panorama-terrace; Alexanderplatz 7; €4; ⏰noon-10pm Apr-Oct, to 6pm Nov-Mar, weather permitting; Ⓤ Alexanderplatz, 🚇Alexanderplatz)

Nikolaiviertel AREA

9 MAP P64, D4

Commissioned by the East German government to celebrate Berlin's 750th birthday, the twee Nicholas Quarter is a half-hearted attempt at recreating the city's medieval birthplace around its oldest surviving building, the 1230 Nikolaikirche. The maze of cobbled lanes is worth a quick stroll, while several olde-worlde-style restaurants provide sustenance. (btwn Rathausstrasse, Breite Strasse, Spandauer Strasse & Mühlendamm; admission free; Ⓤ Klosterstrasse)

Eating

Dolores CALIFORNIAN €

10 MAP P64, D1

Dolores hasn't lost a step since introducing the California-style burrito to Berlin. Pick your favourites from among the marinated meats (or tofu), rice, beans, veggies, cheeses and homemade salsas, and the cheerful staff will build it on the spot. Goes perfectly with an *agua fresca* (Mexican-style lemonade). (☎030-2809 9597; www.dolores-online.de; Rosa-Luxemburg-Strasse 7; burritos from €4.50; ⏰11.30am-10pm Mon-Sat, 1-10pm Sun; 🛜✓; 🚌100, 200, 🚇Alexanderplatz, Ⓤ Alexanderplatz)

Ishin JAPANESE €€

11 MAP P64, C2

The newest outpost of this local sushi chain dishes up freshly prepared and good-value sushi along with *donburi* rice bowls and dishes prepared in the bamboo steamer. Prices for sushi menus drop during Happy Hour, which runs all day Wednesday and Saturday and

until 4pm on other opening days.
(📞030-2352 2762; www.ishin.de;
Litfass-Platz 1; sushi platter €8.50-21,
bowl €5.60-12.20; ⏰noon-9.30pm
Mon-Sat; 🚊M1, Ⓢ Hackescher Markt)

Brauhaus Georgbräu GERMAN €€

12 🍴 MAP P64, C4

Solidly on the tourist track, this old-
style gastropub churns out its own
light and dark Georg-Bräu, which
can even be ordered by the metre
(12 glasses at 0.2L). In winter, the
woodsy beer hall is perfect for
tucking into hearty Berlin-style
fare, while in summer tables in the
riverside beer garden are golden.
(📞030-242 4244; www.brauhaus-
georgbraeu.de; Spreeufer 4; mains €6-
15; ⏰noon-midnight; Ⓤ Klosterstrasse)

Hofbräuhaus Berlin GERMAN €€

13 🍴 MAP P64, E1

Popular with coach tourists and
field-tripping teens, this giant beer
hall with 2km of wooden benches
does not have the patina of the
Munich original but at least it
serves the same litre-size mugs of
beer and big plates piled high with
gut-busting German fare. (📞030-
679 665 520; www.hofbraeu-wirtshaus.
de/berlin; Karl-Liebknecht-Strasse 30;
sausages €6-9, mains €11-20; ⏰10am-
1am Sun-Thu, to 2am Fri & Sat; 👶;
Ⓢ Alexanderplatz, Ⓤ Alexanderplatz)

Zur Letzten Instanz GERMAN €€

14 🍴 MAP P64, E4

With its folksy Old Berlin charm,
this rustic eatery has been an

enduring hit since 1621 and has
fed everyone from Napoleon to
Beethoven to Angela Merkel.
Although the restaurant is now
tourist-geared, the food quality is
reassuringly high when it comes
to such local rib-stickers as grilled
pork knuckle or meatballs in caper
sauce. (📞030-242 5528; www.
zurletzteninstanz.de; Waisenstrasse
14-16; mains €13-23; ⏰noon-1am Tue-
Sat, noon-10pm Sun; Ⓤ Klosterstrasse)

Drinking

Braufactum Berlin CRAFT BEER

15 🍺 MAP P64, E1

With its urban-contempo looks and
big terrace, this concept-driven
craft beer outpost shakes up the
gastro wasteland of Alexanderplatz. Aside from the dozen house
brews like the subtly sweet-bitter
India Pale Ale Progusta and the
whisky-barrel-matured Barrel 1,
the blackboard menu also features
suds from other breweries like
Mikkeler and Firestone Walker.
Elevated pub grub helps keep
brains in balance. (📞030-8471 2959;
www.braufactum.de; Memhardstrasse
1; ⏰noon-midnight Sun-Thu, to 2am
Fri & Sat; 🚌100, Ⓤ Alexanderplatz,
Ⓢ Alexanderplatz)

House of Weekend CLUB

16 🍺 MAP P64, F2

This veteran electro club has a
high-flying location on the 15th
floor of a socialist-era office building and often has big-name local
and international DJs helming

Humboldt Forum: Berlin's Upcoming Cultural Hub

Set to open in 2019 or 2020, the **Humboldt Forum** (www.humboldt forum.com; Schlossplatz; 100, 200, TXL, ⓤKlosterstrasse) will be Berlin's new cultural hub set within an exact replica of the baroque Berlin City Palace, but with a modern interior. Admission to all permanent exhibits is expected to be free for the first three years.

Although barely damaged in WWII, the grand palace where Prussian rulers had made their home since 1443 was blown up by East Germany's government in 1950 to drop the final curtain on Prussian and Nazi rule. To emphasise the point, the new communist rulers built their own modernist parliament – called Palast der Repubilk (Palace of the Republic) – on top of the ruins 26 years later. Riddled with asbestos, it too had a date with the wrecking ball in 2006.

When it opens, the Humboldt Forum will house the **Museum of Ethnology and** the **Museum of Asian Art** as well as the **Berlin Ausstellung** (Berlin Exhibit), which will focus on Berlin's global links and examine such issues as migration, war, fashion and revolution. Films, lectures and other events will complement the permanent exhibits.

its decks. In summer, the action expands to the rooftop terrace for sundowners, private cabanas and 360° views. (🏠 reservations 0152 2429 3140; www.houseofweekend. berlin; Am Alexanderplatz 5; ⏰11pm-6am Fri & Sat, roof garden from 7pm, weather permitting; ⓢAlexanderplatz, ⓤAlexanderplatz)

Shopping

Alexa   MALL

17 🔒 MAP P64, F3

Power shoppers love this XXL mall, which cuts a rose-hued presence near Alexanderplatz and features the predictable range of high-street retailers. Good food court for a bite on the run. (🏠030-269 3400; www.alexacentre. com; Grunerstrasse 20; ⏰10am-9pm Mon-Sat; ⓢAlexanderplatz, ⓤAlexanderplatz)

Galeria Kaufhof   DEPARTMENT STORE

18 🔒 MAP P64, E2

A full makeover by the late Josef Paul Kleihues turned this former GDR-era department store into a glitzy retail cube, complete with a glass-domed light court and a sleek travertine skin that glows green at night. There's little you won't find on the five football-field-size floors, including a gourmet supermarket on the ground floor. (🏠030-247 430; www.galeria-kaufhof. de; Alexanderplatz 9; ⏰9.30am-8pm Mon-Wed, to 10pm Thu-Sat; ⓢAlexanderplatz, ⓤAlexanderplatz)

Explore ◈
Potsdamer Platz

This new quarter, forged from ground once bisected by the Berlin Wall, is a showcase of fabulous contemporary architecture and home to big cinemas and shopping. Culture lovers should not skip the Kulturforum museums, especially the Gemäldegalerie, which sits right next to the world-class Berliner Philharmonie. It hugs the leafy Tiergarten whose rambling paths, hidden monuments and beer gardens make for a perfect sightseeing break.

Whiz up to the Panoramapunkt (p77) for coffee and bird's-eye views of Berlin's landmarks, then saunter over to the Gemäldegalerie (p72) for a rendezvous with Rembrandt and Co. Head back to Potsdamer Platz for lunch at Ki-Nova (p87) and a closer look at the Sony Center (p77) before delving first into the darkness of the Nazi era at the Topographie des Terrors (p85) and then the Cold War at Checkpoint Charlie (p85). Cheer up with craft beer at BRLO Brwhouse (p90) before treating your ears to classical sounds of the Berliner Philharmoniker (p91) or your palate to progressive Thai at Kin Dee (p87).

Getting There & Around

🚌 The 200 comes through en route from Bahnhof Zoologischer Garten and Alexanderplatz; M41 links the Hauptbahnhof with Kreuzberg and Neukölln via Potsdamer Platz; and the M29 connects with Checkpoint Charlie.

Ⓢ S1 and S2 link Potsdamer Platz with Unter den Linden and the Scheunenviertel.

Ⓤ U2 stops at Potsdamer Platz and Mendelssohn-Bartholdy-Park.

Potsdamer Platz Map on p84

Top Sight 📷
Gemäldegalerie

The Gemäldegalerie (Gallery of Old Masters) ranks among the world's finest and most comprehensive collections of European art from the 13th to the 18th centuries. Expect to feast your eyes on masterpieces by Titian, Goya, Botticelli, Holbein, Gainsborough, Canaletto, Hals, Rubens, Vermeer and many other Old Masters. The gallery also hosts high-profile visiting exhibits featuring works from the great artists of this period.

◎ MAP P84, A2

www.smb.museum/gg

Matthäikirchplatz

adult/concession/under 18 €10/5/free

🕑10am-6pm Tue, Wed & Fri, to 8pm Thu, 11am-6pm Sat & Sun

S Potsdamer Platz,
U Potsdamer Platz

Fountain of Youth (1546)

ROOM III

Lucas Cranach the Elder's poignant painting illustrates humankind's yearning for eternal youth. Old crones plunge into a pool of water and emerge as dashing hotties – this fountain would surely put plastic surgeons out of business. The transition is reflected in the landscape, which is stark and craggy on the left, and lush and fertile on the right.

Portrait of Hieronymus Holzschuher (1526)

ROOM 2

Hieronymus Holzschuher was a Nuremberg patrician, a career politician and a strong supporter of the Reformation. He was also a friend of one of the greatest German Renaissance painters, Albrecht Dürer. In this portrait, which shows its sitter at age 57, the artist brilliantly lasers in on Holzschuher's features with utmost precision, down to the furrows, wrinkles and thinning hair.

Portrait of a Young Lady (1470)

ROOM 4

Berlin's own 'Mona Lisa' may not be as famous as the real thing but she's quite intriguing nonetheless. Who is this woman with the almond-shaped eyes and porcelain skin who gazes straight at us with a blend of sadness and skepticism? This famous portrait is a key work by Petrus Christus and his only one depicting a woman.

Dutch Proverbs (1559)

ROOM 7

In this moralistic yet humorous painting, Dutch Renaissance painter Pieter Bruegel the Elder illustrates more than 100 proverbs and idioms in a single seaside village scene. While some emphasise the absurdity of human behaviour, others unmask its imprudence and sinfulness. Some sayings are still in use today, among them

★ Top Tips

○ Take advantage of the excellent free audioguide to get the low-down on selected works.

○ Note that the room numbering system is quite confusing as both Latin (I, II, III) and Arabic numbers (1, 2, 3) are used.

○ Paintings are occasionally rehung, so rooms numbers listed here are subject to change.

○ A tour of all 72 rooms covers almost 2km, so allow at least a couple of hours for your visit and wear comfortable shoes.

○ Admission is free to anyone under 18.

✕ Take a Break

The upstairs museum cafeteria has a salad bar, precooked meals (around €6) and hot and cold beverages.

'swimming against the tide' and 'armed to the teeth'.

Malle Babbe (1633)

ROOM 13

Frans Hals ingeniously captures the character and vitality of his subject, 'Crazy Barbara', with free-wielding brushstrokes. Hals met the woman with the almost demonic laugh in the workhouse for the mentally ill where his son Pieter was also a resident. The tin mug and owl are symbols of Babbe's fondness for tipple.

Mennonite Minister Cornelius Claesz Anslo (1641)

ROOM X

A masterpiece in the gallery's prized Rembrandt collection, this large-scale canvas shows the cloth merchant and Mennonite preacher Anslo in conversation with his wife. The huge open Bible and his gesturing hand sticking out in almost 3D style from the centre of the painting are meant to emphasise the strength of his religious convictions.

Woman with a Pearl Necklace (1662-64)

ROOM 18

No, it's not the Girl with a Pearl Earring of book and movie fame, but it's still one of Jan Vermeer's most famous paintings: a young woman studies herself in the mirror while fastening a pearl necklace. A top dog among Dutch Realist painters, Vermeer mesmerises viewers by beautifully capturing this intimate moment with characteristic soft brushstrokes.

Gemäldegalerie

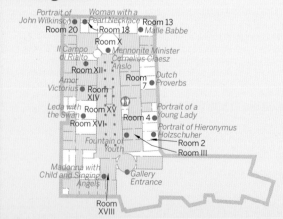

Portrait of John Wilkinson (1775)

ROOM 20

Works by Thomas Gainsborough are rarely seen outside the UK, which is what makes this portrait of British industrialist John Wilkinson so special. Nicknamed 'Iron Mad Wilkinson' for pioneering the making and use of cast iron, here he is – somewhat ironically – shown in a natural setting, almost blending in with his surroundings.

Il Campo di Rialto (1758-63)

ROOM XII

Giovanni Antonio Canal, aka Canaletto, studied painting in the workshop of his theatre-set-designer father. Here he depicts the Campo di Rialto, the arcaded main market square of his hometown, Venice, with stunning precision and perspective. Note the goldsmith shops on the left, the wig-wearing merchants in the centre and the stores selling paintings and furniture on the right.

Amor Victorius (1602-03)

ROOM XIV

That's quite a cheeky fellow peering down on viewers, isn't it? Wearing nothing but a mischievous grin and a pair of black angel wings, with a fistful of arrows, this Amor means business. In this famous painting, Caravaggio shows off his amazing talent at depicting objects with near-photographic realism achieved by his ingeniously theatrical use of light and shadow.

Leda with the Swan (1532)

ROOM XV

Judging by her blissed-out expression, Leda is having a fine time with that swan who, according to Greek mythology, is none other than Zeus himself. The erotically charged nature of this painting by Italian Renaissance artist Correggio apparently so incensed its one-time owner Louis of Orléans that he cut off Leda's head with a knife. It was later restored.

Madonna with Child & Singing Angels (1477)

ROOM XVIII

Renaissance artist Sandro Botticelli's circular painting (a format called a tondo) is a symmetrical composition showing Mary at the centre flanked by two sets of four wingless angels. It's an intimate moment that shows the Virgin tenderly embracing – perhaps even about to breastfeed – her child. The white lilies are symbols of her purity.

Top Sight 📷
Potsdamer Platz

The rebirth of the historic Potsdamer Platz was Europe's biggest building project of the 1990s, a showcase of urban renewal masterminded by such top international architects as Renzo Piano and Helmut Jahn. An entire city quarter sprouted on terrain once bifurcated by the Berlin Wall and today houses offices, theatres and cinemas, hotels, apartments and museums.

🎯 **MAP P84, C2**

Alte Potsdamer Strasse

🚌200, Ⓢ Potsdamer Platz, Ⓤ Potsdamer Platz

Sony Center

Designed by Helmut Jahn, the visually dramatic **Sony Center** (pictured left; Potsdamer Strasse) is fronted by a 26-floor, glass-and-steel tower that integrates architectural relics from the pre-war Potsdamer Platz. A tentlike glass roof with supporting beams radiating like bicycle spokes canopies a central cafe-ringed plaza.

Museum für Film und Fernsehen

From silent movies to sci-fi, Germany's long and illustrious film history gets the star treatment at the **Museum für Film und Fernsehen** (☏030-300 9030; www.deutsche-kinemathek.de; Potsdamer Strasse 2; adult/concession €8/5, free 4-8pm Thu; ◷10am-6pm Wed & Fri-Mon, to 8pm Thu). Major themes include pioneers and early divas, silent-era classics such as Fritz Lang's *Metropolis*, Leni Riefenstahl's groundbreaking Nazi-era documentary *Olympia*, German exiles in Hollywood and diva extraordinaire Marlene Dietrich.

Panoramapunkt

A lift yo-yoes up the postmodern Kollhoff Tower to the **Panoramapunkt** (☏030-2593 7080; www.panoramapunkt.de; Potsdamer Platz 1; adult/concession €7.50/6, without wait €11.50/9; ◷10am-8pm Apr-Oct, to 6pm Nov-Mar) viewing platform. From a lofty 100m, you can pinpoint the sights, make a java stop in the 1930s-style cafe, enjoy sunset from the terrace and check out the history exhibit.

Daimler Contemporary Berlin

Ring the bell to be buzzed into the free **Daimler Contemporary Berlin** (☏030-2594 1420; www.art.daimler.com; Alte Potsdamer Strasse 5, Weinhaus Huth, 4th fl; admission free; ◷11am-6pm), which showcases international abstract, conceptual and minimalist art. It's on the top floor of the 1912 **Weinhaus Huth**, one of the first steel-frame buildings in town and the only Potsdamer Platz structure that survived WWII intact.

★ **Top Tip**

○ Check out the Berlin Wall segments outside the Potsdamer Platz S-Bahn station entrance.

○ From September to June, free classical concerts draw music lovers to the nearby Berliner Philharmonie (p91) at 1pm on Tuesdays.

○ Admission to the Museum für Film und Fernsehen is free from 4pm to 8pm Thursdays.

○ An original Berlin Wall guard tower is just a short walk away on Erna-Berger-Strasse (off Stresemannstrasse).

✕ **Take a Break**

○ For fantastic ice cream, head to Caffe e Gelato (p88) in the Potsdamer Platz Arkaden.

○ Restore energy with a superfood lunch at Ki-Nova (p87), an upbeat cafe with sunny sidewalk tables.

Top Sight 📷
Jüdisches Museum

In a landmark building by Daniel Libeskind, Berlin's Jewish Museum has, since 2001, chronicled the trials and triumphs of 2000 years of German history, as seen through the eyes of the Jewish minority. The exhibit smoothly navigates all major periods, from the Middle Ages via the Enlightenment to the community's current renaissance.

◎ MAP P84, F4

www.jmberlin.de

Lindenstrasse 9-14

adult/concession €8/3, audioguide €3

🕑10am-8pm

Ⓤ Hallesches Tor, Kochstrasse

The Building

Libeskind's architectural masterpiece (which he titled *Between the Lines*) is essentially a 3D metaphor for the tortured history of the Jewish people. Its zigzag shape symbolises a broken Star of David; its silvery titanium-zinc walls are sharply angled; and instead of windows, there are only small gashes piercing the building's gleaming facade.

The Axes

The museum consists of two buildings. The entrance is via a stately baroque structure that once housed the Prussian supreme court. From here a steep, dark and winding staircase leads down to the Libeskind building and three intersecting walkways (called 'axes') that are a visual allegory for the fates of Jews in the 20th century: death, exile and continuity. Only the latter axis leads to the actual exhibits, but it too is a cumbersome journey up a sloping walkway and several steep flights of stairs.

Art Installations

The Jewish Museum is peppered with art installations, including the extraordinary **Shalekhet – Fallen Leaves** by the late Menashe Kadishma. More than 10,000 open-mouthed faces cut from rusty iron plates lie arbitrarily scattered on the floor in an ocean of silent screams. The haunting effect is exacerbated by the space itself, a cold and claustrophobic 'void'. Also note Dresden-born artist Via Lewandowsky's **Gallery of the Missing**, which consists of five black glass sculptures set up throughout the exhibition floor near these voids. Each contains acoustic descriptions of missing or destroyed objects relating to German-Jewish culture , such as the *Encyclopaedia Judaica*, whose completion came to an abrupt halt in 1934.

★ **Top Tip**

○ Tickets are also valid for reduced admission on the same day and the next two days to the Berlinische Galerie (p87), a survey of 150 years of Berlin art, located just 500m away.

○ Rent the audioguide (€3) for a more in-depth experience.

○ Free themed tours (in German) take place at 3pm on Saturday and at 11am and 2pm on Sunday.

○ Budget at least two hours to visit the museum, plus extra time to go through the airport-style entrance security checks.

✕ **Take a Break**

For a refuelling stop, pop by the museum's **Café Schmus** (☏ 030-2579 6751; www.koflerkompanie.com; Lindenstrasse 9, Jüdisches Museum; dishes €5.50-8; ⊙10am-10pm Mon, to 8pm Tue-Sun; Ⓤ Kochstrasse, Hallesches Tor) for modern takes on traditional Jewish cuisine.

Walking Tour 🥾

A Leisurely Tiergarten Stroll

Berlin's rulers used to hunt boar and pheasants in the rambling Tiergarten until garden architect Peter Lenné landscaped the grounds in the 18th century. Today it's one of the world's largest urban parks, popular for strolling, jogging, picnicking, Frisbee tossing and sunbathing. Walking across the entire park takes at least an hour, but even a shorter stroll has its rewards.

Walk Facts

Start Brandenburg Gate
Ⓤ Brandenburger Tor,
Ⓢ Brandenburger Tor

End Potsdamer Platz,
Ⓤ Potsdamer Platz,
Ⓢ Potsdamer Platz

Length 4km; two hours

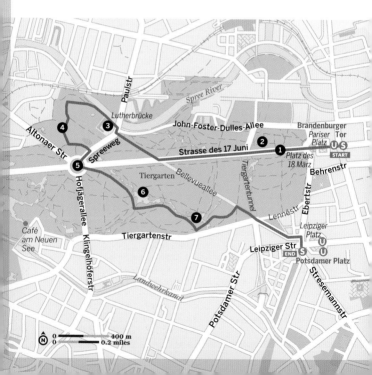

❶ Strasse des 17 Juni

The broad boulevard bisecting Tiergarten was named Street of 17 June in honour of the victims of the bloodily quashed 1953 workers' uprising in East Berlin. Back in the 16th century, the road linked two royal palaces; it was doubled in width and turned into a triumphal road under Hitler.

❷ Sowjetisches Ehrenmal

Berlin lay in ruins when the imposing **Soviet War Memorial** was dedicated in November 1945. It is one of three in the city that honours the 80,000 Soviet soldiers who died in the Battle of Berlin, including the 2000 buried behind its colonnades. The memorial's entrance is flanked by two Russian T-34 tanks, said to have been the first to enter the city.

❸ Schloss Bellevue

A succession of German presidents have made their home in snowy-white **Bellevue Palace** on the edge of the Tiergarten. The neoclassical pile was originally a pad for the youngest brother of King Frederick the Great. It became a school under Kaiser Wilhelm II and a museum of ethnology under the Nazis. It's closed to the public.

❹ Teehaus im Englischen Garten

In a hidden corner of Tiergarten, this reed-thatched **teahouse** (☎030-3948 0400; www.teehaus-tiergarten.com; Altonaer Strasse 2; mains €9-19.50; ☉noon-11pm Tue-Sat, from 10am Sun; ☐100, ⑤Bellevue, Ⓤ Hansaplatz) is an idyllic spot, especially in summer when the beer garden gets packed. Free concerts on Sundays.

❺ Siegessäule

Engulfed by roundabout traffic, the 1873 **Victory Column** was erected to celebrate Prussian military victories and is now a prominent symbol of Berlin's gay community. The gilded woman on top represents the goddess of victory and is featured prominently in the Wim Wenders movie *Wings of Desire*. The column originally stood in front of the Reichstag until the Nazis moved it here in 1938. Climb to the top to appreciate the park's dimensions.

❻ Rousseauinsel

One of Tiergarten's most idyllic spots is the **Rousseauinsel**, a teensy island in a placid pond that's a memorial to 18th-century French philosopher Jean-Jacques Rousseau. It was designed to resemble his actual burial site on an island near Paris. Look for the stone pillar.

❼ Luiseninsel

Another enchanting place, **Luiseninsel** is a tranquil gated garden brimming with statues and resplendent with seasonal flower beds. It was created after Napoleon's occupying troops left town in 1808 in celebration of the return from exile of the royal couple King Friedrich Wilhelm III and Queen Luise.

Walking Tour 🥾

Walking the Wall

Construction of the Berlin Wall began shortly after midnight on 13 August 1961. For the next 28 years this grim barrier divided a city and its people, becoming the most visible symbol of the Cold War. By now the city's halves have visually merged so perfectly that it takes a keen eye to tell East from West. To give you a sense of the division, this walk follows the most central section of the Berlin Wall.

Walk Facts

Start Checkpoint Charlie; Ⓤ Kochstrasse/ Checkpoint Charlie

End Parlament der Baume; Ⓤ Bundestag

Length 3km; two hours

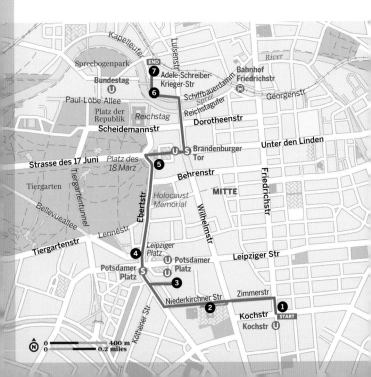

❶ Checkpoint Charlie

As the third Allied checkpoint, **Checkpoint Charlie** (p85) got its name from the third letter in the NATO phonetic alphabet. Weeks after the Wall was built, US and Soviet tanks faced off here in one of the tensest moments of the Cold War.

❷ Niederkirchner Strasse

Along Niederkirchner Strasse looms a 200m-long section of the original **outer border wall**. Scarred by souvenir hunters, it's now protected by a fence.The border strip was very narrow here, with the inner wall abutting such buildings as the former **Nazi Air Force Ministry** on the corner of Niederkirchner Strasse and Wilhelmstrasse.

❸ Border Watchtower

Imagine what it was like to be a Berlin Wall border guard when climbing up the iron ladder of one of the few remaining **watchtowers**. The octagonal observation perch of this 1969 model was particularly cramped and later replaced by larger square towers. After a thorough restoration by a nonprofit group, the tower is now open to the public.

❹ Potsdamer Platz

Potsdamer Platz used to be a massive no-man's land bisected by the Wall and a 'death strip' several hundred metres wide. Outside the northern S-Bahn station entrance are a few **Berlin Wall segments**.

❺ Brandenburg Gate

The **Brandenburg Gate** (p42) was where construction of the Wall began. Many heads of state gave speeches in front of it, including former US president Ronald Reagan who, in 1987, uttered the famous words: 'Mr Gorbachev – tear down this wall!'

❻ Art Installations

In the basement of the **Marie-Elisabeth-Lüders-Haus** (www.bundestag.de; Schiffbauerdamm; admission free; ⊙galleries 11am-5pm Tue-Sun; **S** Hauptbahnhof, **U** Bundestag, Hauptbahnhof), an art installation by Ben Wagin runs along the original course of the Berlin Wall. It consists of original segments, each painted with a year and the number of people killed at the Wall in that year. Enter from the Spree promenade. If it's closed, you can easily you can easily sneak a peak through the window of this government building that houses the parliamentary library.

❼ Parlament der Bäume

Wagin also masterminded the **Parliament of Trees**, a quiet garden and environmental art installation. It consists not only of trees but of memorial stones, pictures, text and 58 original pieces of the Wall inscribed with the names of 258 victims.

Potsdamer Platz

For reviews see

◎ Top Sights	p72
◉ Sights	p85
✕ Eating	p87
🍷 Drinking	p90
🎭 Entertainment	p91
🛍 Shopping	p91

TIERGARTEN

Tiergarten

Musikinstrumenten-Museum

Kunstgewerbemuseum

Gemäldegalerie

Sigismundstr

Gedenkstätte Deutscher Widerstand

Matthäikirchplatz

Kupferstichkabinett

Kulturforum

Landwehrkanal

Reichpietschufer

Schöneberger Ufer

Lützowstr

Lützowstr

9

17

12

15

9

Pohlstr

Kurfürstenstr

Potsdamer Str

In den Ministergärten

Kemperplatz

Vossstr

Leipziger Str

Potsdamer Platz

Potsdamer Platz

19

Am Park

14

7

Bellevuestr

Ben-Gurion-Str

Gabriele-Tergit-Promenade

Linkstr

Alte Potsdamer Str

Marlene-Dietrich-Platz

Potsdamer Brücke

11

Stresemannstr

Köthener Str

Dessauer Str

10

Mendelssohn-Bartholdy-Park

13

Gleisdreieck

Flottwellstr

Schöneberger Ufer

Tempelhofer Ufer

Hallesches Ufer

Möckernstr

WESTERN KREUZBERG

Anhalter Bahnhof

16

Anhalter Str

Askanischer Platz

Martin-Gropius-Bau

Topographie des Terrors

4

Niederkirchner Str

Stresemannstr

Wilhelmstr

Mohrenstr

Taubenstr

Friedrichstadtpassagen

Stadtmitte

Leipziger Str

Friedrichstr

Mauerstr

Checkpoint Charlie

2

Schützenstr

Zimmerstr

Markgrafenstr

Charlottenstr

Rudi-Dutschke-Str

Kochstr

Kochstr

8

KREUZBERG

Lindenstr

Jüdisches Museum

Ritterstr

Berlinische Galerie

5

Franz-Klühs-Str

400 m

0.2 miles

Sights

Topographie des Terrors

MUSEUM

1  MAP P84, D2

In the spot where the most feared institutions of Nazi Germany (including the Gestapo headquarters and the SS central command) once stood, this compelling exhibit chronicles the stages of terror and persecution, puts a face on the perpetrators and details the impact these brutal institutions had on all of Europe. A second exhibit outside zeroes in on how life changed for Berlin and its people after the Nazis made it their capital. (Topography of Terror; ☏030-2545 0950; www.topographie.de; Niederkirchner Strasse 8; admission free; ◷10am-8pm, grounds close at dusk or 8pm at the latest; ☒M41, ⑤Potsdamer Platz, Ⓤ Potsdamer Platz)

Checkpoint Charlie HISTORIC SITE

2  MAP P84, E2

Checkpoint Charlie was the principal gateway for foreigners and diplomats between the two Berlins from 1961 to 1990. Unfortunately, this potent symbol of the Cold War has degenerated into a tacky tourist trap, though a free **open-air exhibit** that illustrates milestones in Cold War history is one redeeming aspect. (cnr Zimmerstrasse & Friedrichstrasse; admission free; ◷24hr; Ⓤ Kochstrasse)

Checkpoint Charlie

Kulturforum Museums

In addition to the famous Gemäldegalerie (p72) and Neue National-galerie (which is closed for renovations), the Kulturforum encompasses three other top-rated museums: the **Kupferstichkabinett** (Museum of Prints & Drawings; Map p84, A2; ☏030-266 424 242; www.smb.museum/kk; Matthäikirchplatz; adult/concession €6/3; ⏰10am-6pm Tue-Fri, 11am-6pm Sat & Sun; ☒M29, M48, M85, 200, Ⓢ Potsdamer Platz, Ⓤ Potsdamer Platz) with prints and drawings dating from the 14th century; the **Musikinstrumenten-Museum** (Musical Instruments Museum; Map p84, B1; ☏030-2548 1178; www.simpk.de; Tiergartenstrasse 1, enter via Ben-Gurion-Strasse; adult/concession/under 18 €6/3/free; ⏰9am-5pm Tue, Wed & Fri, to 8pm Thu, to 5pm Sat & Sun; ☒200, Ⓢ Potsdamer Platz, Ⓤ Potsdamer Platz) with rare historical instruments; and the **Kunstgewerbemuseum** (Museum of Decorative Arts; Map p84, A1; ☏030-266 424 242; www.smb.museum; Matthäikirchplatz; adult/concession/under 18 €8/4/free; ⏰10am-6pm Tue-Fri, 11am-6pm Sat & Sun; ☒M29, M48, M85, 200, Ⓢ Potsdamer Platz, Ⓤ Potsdamer Platz), with its prized collection of arts and crafts. A day ticket valid for all Kulturforum museums costs €12.

Gedenkstätte Deutscher Widerstand
MEMORIAL

3 ◉ MAP P84, A2

This memorial exhibit on German Nazi resistance occupies the rooms where high-ranking officers led by Claus Schenk Graf von Stauffenberg plotted the assassination attempt on Hitler on 20 July 1944. There's a memorial in the courtyard where the main conspirators were shot right after the failed coup, a story poignantly retold in the 2008 movie *Valkyrie*. (German Resistance Memorial Centre; ☏030-2699 5000; www.gdw-berlin.de; Stauffenbergstrasse 13-14, enter via courtyard; admission free; ⏰9am-6pm Mon-Wed & Fri, to 8pm Thu, 10am-6pm Sat & Sun; ☒M29, M48, Ⓢ Potsdamer Platz, Ⓤ Potsdamer Platz, Kurfürstenstrasse)

Martin-Gropius-Bau
GALLERY

4 ◉ MAP P84, D2

With its mosaics, terracotta reliefs and airy atrium, this Italian Renaissance–style exhibit space named for its architect (Bauhaus founder Walter Gropius' great-uncle) is a celebrated venue for high-calibre art and cultural exhibits. Whether it's a David Bowie retrospective, the latest works of Ai Weiwei or an ethnological exhibit on the mysteries of Angkor Wat, it's bound to be well curated and utterly fascinating. (☏030-254 860; www.gropiusbau.de; Niederkirchner Strasse 7; cost varies, usually €10-12, under 16 free; ⏰10am-7pm Wed-Mon; ☒M41, Ⓢ Potsdamer Platz, Ⓤ Potsdamer Platz)

Berlinische Galerie

GALLERY

5 ⊙ MAP P84, F3

This gallery in a converted glass warehouse is a superb spot for taking stock of Berlin's art scene since 1870. Temporary exhibits occupy the ground floor, from where two floating staircases lead upstairs to selections from the permanent collection, which is especially strong when it comes to Dada, New Objectivity, Eastern European avant-garde, and art created since reunification in 1990. (Berlin Museum of Modern Art, Photography & Architecture; ☏030-7890 2600; www.berlinischegalerie. de; Alte Jakobstrasse 124-128; adult/concession/child under 18 €8/5/free; ⊙10am-6pm Wed-Mon; Ⓤ Hallesches Tor, Kochstrasse)

Eating

Kin Dee

THAI €€€

6 ⊗ MAP P84, A3

One of most buzzed-about new restaurants on Potsdamer Strasse is Dalad Kambhu's lair Kin Dee, where she fearlessly catapults classic Thai dishes into the 21st century, and even adapts them by using locally grown ingredients. One constant is her signature homemade spice pastes that beautifully underline the aromatic dimensions of each dish. (☏030-215 5294; www. kindeeberlin.com; Lützowstrasse 81; tasting menu €45; ⊙6-10pm Tue-Sat; 🛜; Ⓤ Kurfürstenstrasse)

Ki-Nova

INTERNATIONAL €€

7 ⊗ MAP P84, B1

The name of this lunchtime favourite hints at the concept: 'ki' is Japanese for energy and 'nova' Latin for new. 'New energy' in this case translates into health-focused yet comforting bites starring global and regional superfoods from kale to cranberries. The contempo interior radiates urban warmth with heavy plank tables, black tiled bar, movie stills and floor-to-ceiling windows. (☏030-2546 4860; www.ki-nova.de; Potsdamer Strasse 2; mains €9-17; ⊙11.30am-11pm Mon-Fri, 1-11pm Sat, 1-9pm Sun; 🛜🍴; 🚌200, Ⓤ Potsdamer Platz, Ⓢ Potsdamer Platz)

Nobelhart & Schmutzig

INTERNATIONAL €€€

8 ⊗ MAP P84, E3

'Brutally local' is the motto at the Michelin-starred restaurant of star sommelier Billy Wagner. All ingredients hail – without exception – from producers in and around Berlin and the nearby Baltic Sea – hence, no pepper or lemons. The seating and service quite literally break down boundaries, as guests are seated along the kitchen counter to observe staff fussing over their 10-course dinner. (☏030-2594 0610; www. nobelhartundschmutzig.com; Friedrichstrasse 218; 10-course menu Tue & Wed €95, Thu-Sat €120; ⊙6.30pm-midnight Tue-Sat; Ⓤ Kochstrasse)

Panama INTERNATIONAL €€

9 ✕ MAP P84, A4

On balmy nights, a glass of rosé and a grazing session in the courtyard of this art-crowd darling will likely transport you, maybe not quite to Panama, but certainly away from Berlin's urban velocity. Elevating standards on up-and-coming Potsdamer Strasse, the produce-focused small-plate menu – divided into raw, leaves, grains, meat and fish – is innovative and sometimes brilliantly experimental. (030-983 208 435; www.oh-panama.com; Potsdamer Strasse 91; dishes €9-19; 6-11pm Wed-Sat; Kurfürstenstrasse)

Mabuhay INDONESIAN €

10 ✕ MAP P84, C3

Tucked into a concrete courtyard, this hole-in-the-wall scores a one for looks and a 10 for the food. Usually packed (especially at lunchtime), it delivers Indonesian food with as much authenticity as possible. The heat meter has been adjusted for German tastes, but the spicing of such dishes as gado gado or curry rendang is still feisty and satisfying. (030-265 1867; www.mabuhay.juisyfood.com; Köthener Strasse 28; mains €6-13; noon-3pm Mon-Fri, 5-9.30pm Mon-Sat; Mendelssohn-Bartholdy-Park)

Caffe e Gelato ICE CREAM €

11 ✕ MAP P84, C2

Traditional Italian-style ice cream gets a 21st-century twist at this huge cafe on the upper floor of the **Potsdamer Platz Arkaden** (Map p84, C2; 030-255 9270; www.potsdamerplatz.de/potsdamer-platz-arkaden; Alte Potsdamer Strasse 7; 10am-9pm Mon-Sat; Potsdamer Platz, Potsdamer Platz) mall. Among the homemade creamy concoctions are organic and sugar-, gluten- and lactose-free varieties in unusual flavours, including yoghurt-walnut-fig and almond crunch. (030-2529 7832; www.caffe-e-gelato.de; Alte Potsdamer Strasse 7, Potsdamer Platz Arkaden; scoops €1.60-2.20; 10am-10.30pm Mon-Thu, to 11pm Fri, to 11.30pm Sat, 10.30am-10.30pm Sun; Potsdamer Platz, Potsdamer Platz)

Joseph-Roth-Diele GERMAN €

12 ✕ MAP P84, A3

Named for an Austrian Jewish writer, this wood-panelled salon time warps you back to the 1920s, when Roth used to live next door. Walls decorated with bookshelves and quotations from his works draw a literary, chatty crowd, especially at lunchtime when two daily changing €5 specials (one vegetarian) supplement the hearty menu of German classics. Pay at the counter. (030-2636 9884; www.joseph-roth-diele.de; Potsdamer Strasse 75; mains €7-13; 10am-11pm Mon-Thu, to midnight Fri; Kurfürstenstrasse)

The Berlin Wall

It's more than a tad ironic that Berlin's most popular tourist attraction is one that no longer exists. For 28 years the Berlin Wall, the most potent symbol of the Cold War, divided not only a city but the world.

The Beginning

Shortly after midnight on 13 August 1961, East German soldiers and police began rolling out miles of barbed wire that would soon be replaced with prefabricated concrete slabs. The Wall was a desperate measure launched by the German Democratic Republic (GDR) government to stop the sustained brain and brawn drain the country had experienced since its 1949 founding. Some 3.6 million people had already headed to western Germany, putting the GDR on the brink of economic and political collapse.

The Physical Border

Euphemistically called the 'Anti-Fascist Protection Barrier', the Berlin Wall was continually reinforced and refined. It eventually grew into a complex border-security system consisting of two walls enclosing a 'death strip' riddled with trenches, floodlights, attack dogs, electrified alarm fences and watchtowers staffed by guards with shoot-to-kill orders. Nearly 100,000 GDR citizens tried to escape, many using spectacular contraptions like homemade hot-air balloons or U-boats. There are no exact numbers, but it is believed that hundreds died in the process.

The End

The Wall's demise came as unexpectedly as its creation. Once again the GDR was losing its people in droves, this time via Hungary, which had opened its borders with Austria. Major demonstrations in East Berlin came to a head in early November 1989 when half a million people gathered on Alexanderplatz. Something had to give. It did on 9 November, when a GDR spokesperson mistakenly announced during a press conference on live TV that all travel restrictions to the West would be lifted immediately. Amid scenes of wild partying, the two Berlins came together again. Today, only about 2km of the hated barrier still stands, most famously the 1.3km-long East Side Gallery. In addition, a double row of cobblestones embedded in the pavement and 32 information panels guide visitors along 5.7km of the Wall's course through central Berlin.

Drinking

BRLO Brwhouse
CRAFT BEER

13 🚇 MAP P84, B4

The house-crafted suds flow freely at this shooting star among Berlin's craft breweries. Production, tap-room and restaurant are all housed in 38 shipping containers fronted by a big beer garden with sand box and views of Gleisdreieckpark. Share-able dishes are mostly vegetable-centric, although missing out on the meat prepared to succulent perfection in a smoker would be a shame. (📞0151 7437 4235; www.brlo-brwhouse.de; Schöneberger Strasse 16; mains from €18; ⏰restaurant 5pm-midnight Tue-Fri, noon-midnight Sat & Sun, beer garden noon-midnight Apr-Sep; 🛜👶; ⓊGleisdreieck)

Fragrances
COCKTAIL BAR

14 🚇 MAP P84, C1

Another baby by Berlin cocktail maven Arnd Heissen, Fragrances claims to be the world's first 'perfume bar', a libation station where Heissen mixes potable potions mimicking famous scents. The black-mirrored space in the Ritz-Carlton is like a 3D menu where adventurous drinkers sniff out their favourite from among a row of perfume bottles, then settle back into flocked couches for stylish imbibing. (📞030-337 775 403; www.ritzcarlton.com; Potsdamer Platz 3, Ritz-Carlton; ⏰from 7pm Wed-Sat; 🛜; 🚌200, ⓈPotsdamer Platz, ⓊPotsdamer Platz)

Tiger Bar
BAR

15 🚇 MAP P84, A4

Tiger Bar is a stylish and slightly trippy jewel for curious imbibers. Sustainability is key for bar manager Phum Sila-Trakoon, which is why discarded banana peels from the affiliated Panama (p88) restaurant kitchen may well end up as syrup in his bar. Cocktails range from classic to 'out-there' like Paloma's Fall, a tequila-based potion with grapefruit, buttermilk and sea salt. (📞030-983 208 435; www.oh-panama.com/en/tigerbar; Potsdamer Strasse 191; ⏰8pm-midnight or later Tue-Sat; ⓊKurfürstenstrasse)

Solar Lounge
BAR

16 🚇 MAP P84, D3

Watch the city light up from this 17th-floor glass-walled sky lounge above a posh restaurant. With its dim lighting, soft black leather couches and breathtaking panorama, it's a great spot for sunset drinks or a date night. Getting there aboard an exterior glass lift is half the fun. The entrance is behind the Pit Stop auto shop. (📞0163 765 2700; www.solar-berlin.de; Stresemannstrasse 76; ⏰6pm-2am Sun-Thu, to 3am Fri & Sat; ⓈAnhalter Bahnhof)

Kumpelnest 3000
BAR

17 🚇 MAP P84, A3

A former brothel, this trashy batcave is kitsch enough to feature in a 1940s Shanghai noir thriller. Famous for its debauched all-nighters, it attracts a varied crowd, including the odd celebrity. (📞030-261 6918; www.kumpelnest3000.com; Lützowstrasse 23; 🕐7pm-5am or later; Ⓤ Kurfürstenstrasse)

Entertainment

Berliner Philharmoniker   CLASSICAL MUSIC

18 ⭐ MAP P84, B1

One of the world's most famous orchestras, the Berliner Philharmoniker, is based at the tent-like **Philharmonie**, designed by Hans Scharoun in the 1950s and built in the 1960s. In 2019, Sir Simon Rattle, who's been chief conductor since 2002, will pass on the baton to the Russia-born Kirill Petrenko. Tickets can be booked online. (📞tickets 030-2548 8999; www.berliner-philharmoniker.de; Herbert-von-Karajan-Strasse 1; tickets €21-290; 🚇M29, M48, M85, 200, Ⓢ Potsdamer Platz, Ⓤ Potsdamer Platz)

Shopping

LP12 Mall of Berlin   MALL

19 🔒 MAP P84, C1

This sparkling retail quarter is tailor-made for black-belt mall rats. More than 270 shops vie for your euros, including flagships by Karl Lagerfeld, Hugo Boss, Liebeskind, Marc Cain, Muji and other high-end brands alongside the usual high-street chains like Mango and H&M. Free mobile-phone recharge stations in the basement and on the 2nd floor. (www.mallofberlin.de; Leipziger Platz 12; 🕐10am-9pm Mon-Sat; 🛜; 🚇200, Ⓤ Potsdamer Platz, Ⓢ Potsdamer Platz)

LP12 Mall of Berlin

Walking Tour 🥾

An Afternoon in the Bergmannkiez

*One of Berlin's most charismatic neighbour-
hoods, the Bergmannkiez in western Kreuzberg is
named for its main shopping strip, the Bergmannstrasse, which is chock-a-block with cafes
and indie shops. Above it all 'soars' the Kreuzberg
hill, Berlin's highest natural elevation. If you've got
time, make a detour to nearby Tempelhof Airport,
which has been rebooted as a vast urban park.*

Walk Facts

Start Marheineke
Markthalle; Ⓤ Gneisenau-
strasse (U7)

End Cury 36;
Ⓤ Mehringdamm (U6, U7)

Length 3.5km; two to
three hours

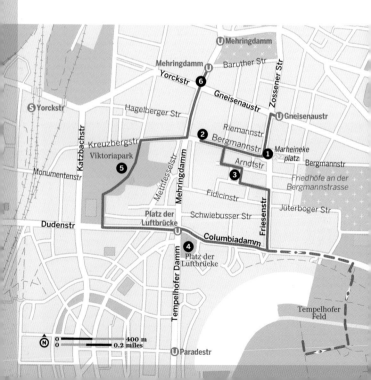

❶ Marheineke Markthalle

The aisles of the renovated 19th-century **Marheineke Markthalle** (www.meine-markthalle.de; Marheinekeplatz; ⊗8am-8pm Mon-Fri, to 6pm Sat; ⓤGneisenaustrasse) brim with vendors plying everything from organic sausages to handmade cheeses, artisanal honey and other bounty.

❷ Pick & Weight Concept Store

Vintage fans love this huge loft **store** (☎030-694 3348; www.kleidermarkt-vintage.de; Bergmannstrasse 102, 1st fl; ⊗11am-8pm Mon-Sat; ⓤMehringdamm) crammed with used clothing going back to the 1960s, all priced by the kilo. Enter via the courtyard.

❸ Chamissoplatz

With its ornate townhouses, cobbled streets, old-timey lanterns and octagonal pissoir, **Chamissoplatz** looks virtually unchanged since the late 19th century, making this square a popular film set.

❹ Luftbrückendenkmal

The **Berlin Airlift Memorial** outside the former Tempelhof Airport honours those who participated in keeping the city fed and free during the 1948–49 Berlin Blockade. The trio of spikes represents the three air corridors used by the Western Allies, while the plinth bears the names of the 79 people who died in this colossal effort.

❺ Viktoriapark

Take a break in this rambling p draped over the 66m-high Kreuz berg hill, home to a vineyard, a waterfall and a pompous memorial commemorating Napoleon's 1815 defeat. In summer, laid-back locals arrive to chill, tan or enjoy drinks at **Golgatha** (☎030-785 2453; www.golgatha-berlin.de; Dudenstrasse 48-64; ⊗9am-late Apr-Aug, weather permitting Sep-Mar; 🚻; Ⓢ Yorckstrasse, ⓤPlatz der Luftbrücke) beer garden.

❻ Curry 36

Day after day, night after night, a motley crowd – cops, cabbies, queens, office jockeys, savvy tourists etc – wait their turn at **Curry 36** (☎030-2580 088 336; www.curry36.de; Mehringdamm 36; snacks €2-6; ⊗9am-5am; ⓤMehringdamm), a top Currywurst purveyor that's been frying 'em up since 1981.

Optional Detour: Tempelhofer Feld

To extend your walk, swing by **Tempelhofer Feld**, a huge untamed urban park on the airfield of decommissioned Tempelhof Airport. Budget an hour or more to explore this noncommercial, creative, open-sky space with a beer garden, art installations, urban gardening, barbecue areas and other fun zones. The main entrance is on Columbiadamm. Entry is free and gates are open from dawn till dusk.

Explore ⊗

Scheunenviertel

The Scheunenviertel (Barn Quarter) packs plenty of charisma into its compact size and is fun to explore by day and night. Walking around you'll constantly stumble upon enchanting surprises: here an idyllic courtyard or bleeding-edge gallery, there a fashion-forward boutique or belle époque ballroom. Since reunification, the area has also reprised its historic role as Berlin's main Jewish quarter.

Start the day with an in-depth study of the Berlin Wall at the Gedenkstätte Berliner Mauer (p96), then head south to the historic Hackesche Höfe (p100) courtyard ensemble. Check out the street art at Haus Schwarzenberg (p102) before embarking on an aimless wander around the area's boutique- and café-lined web of narrow lanes with a stop at the Neue Synagoge (p101). In the afternoon, get your contemporary art fix at the Hamburger Bahnhof (p100) before checking in for a farm-to-table dinner at Katz Orange (p102) or sublime Japanese at Zenkichi (p102). Finish up with cocktails at Buck & Breck (p105) or dancing at endearingly retro Clärchens Ballhaus (p105).

Getting There & Around

Ⓤ Weinmeisterstrasse (U8) is the most central station. Rosenthaler Platz (U8), Rosa-Luxemburg-Platz (U2) and Oranienburger Tor (U6) are closer to Torstrasse.

Ⓢ Hackescher Markt (S5, S7, S75) and Oranienburger Strasse (S1, S2, S25) stations are both good jumping-off points.

🚋 M1 runs from Museumsinsel (Museum Island) to Prenzlauer Berg and stops throughout the Scheunenviertel.

Scheunenviertel Map on p98

Hackesche Höfe (p100) SERGEY KELIN/SHUTTERSTOCK ©

Top Sight 📷
Gedenkstätte Berliner Mauer

For an insightful primer on the Berlin Wall, visit this 1.4km-long outdoor memorial, which explains the physical layout of the barrier and the death strip, how the border fortifications were enlarged and perfected over time and what impact they had on the daily lives of people on both sides of the Wall. The exhibit follows Bernauer Strasse, which was once divided by the Wall, with one side of the street located in West Berlin and the other in East Berlin.

◉ MAP P98, C2

www.berliner-mauer-gedenkstaette.de

admission free

🕓visitor & documentation centre 10am-6pm Tue-Sun, open-air exhibit 8am-10pm daily

Ⓢ Nordbahnhof, Bernauer Strasse, Eberswalder Strasse

National Monument to German Division

Near Ackerstrasse the central memorial to German Division consists of a 70m section of original wall bounded by two rusted steel flanks. Through gaps in a wall, you can espy a reconstructed death strip complete with a guard tower, a security patrol path and the lamps that bathed it in fierce light at night.

Dokumentationszentrum

Across the street from the national monument, the documentation centre provides a concise and engaging overview of the Wall and answers such questions as to why it was built and what led to its collapse. It also uses artefacts, documents and videos to show how it affected daily life on both sides.

Window of Remembrance

Between Gartenstrasse and Ackerstrasse, a wall of photographic portraits gives identity to would-be escapees who lost their lives at the Berlin Wall, one of them only six years young.

Kapelle der Versöhnung

The modern Chapel of Reconciliation stands in the spot of an 1894 brick church detonated in 1985 to make room for a widening of the border strip. A 15-minute remembrance service for Wall victims is held at noon Tuesday to Friday.

Nordbahnhof 'Ghost Station'

The wall also divided the city's transport system. Three lines that originated in West Berlin had to travel along tracks that happened to run beneath East Berlin before returning to stations back on the western side. Trains slowed down but did not stop at these so-called 'ghost stations'. S-Bahn station Nordbahnhof has an exhibit on the subject.

★ Top Tips

o Start your visit in the visitor centre across from Nordbahnhof S-Bahn station and work your way east.

o Pick up a free map and watch the introductory film at the visitors centre.

o If you have limited time, spend it in the first section between Gartenstrasse and Ackerstrasse.

o Enjoy sweeping views of the memorial from the viewing tower of the Documentation Centre near Ackerstrasse.

✗ Take a Break

The Castle (☎ 0151 6767 6757; www.thecastleberlin.de; Invalidenstrasse 129; ⊙ 8am-2am Mon-Fri, 10am-2am Sat & Sun; ☎; ☐ M5, M8, M10, 12, ⑤ Nordbahnhof) is a fine place for coffee and pastries before and craft beer after your sightseeing (or vice versa). Free wi-fi and beer garden.

Scheunenviertel

A   **B**   **C**   **D**

1

For reviews see
⊙	Top Sights	p96
⊙	Sights	p100
⊗	Eating	p102
⊖	Drinking	p105
☆	Entertainment	p106
🔒	Shopping	p107

Streilitzer Str

Bernauer Str

2

Chausseestr

Bergstr

Gedenkstätte
Berliner
Mauer ⊙

Ackerstr

Habersaathstr

Bergstr

Bernauer Str

Gartenstr

Nordbahnhof Ⓢ

Invalidenstr

3

Museum für
Naturkunde
⊙3

Naturkundemuseum
Ⓤ

Eichendorffstr

⊗ 8

Invalidenstr

Schlegelstr

Tieckstr

Gartenstr

Bergstr

Chausseestr

Noralistr

⊖ 19

▲⊙2
▲⊙7

4

Hannoversche Str

Hannoversche Str

Torstr

⊗ 12

KW Institute for
Contemporary Art
6 ⊙

Linienstr

Humboldt-
Universität
zu Berlin

Oranienburger Ⓤ
Tor

Oranienburger Str

Auguststr

13

5

Luisenstr

Friedrichstr

⊗ 9
10 ⊗

25 🔒

Heckmann Höfe

16

Oranienburger Ⓢ
Str

⊙ 5

Johannisstr

Neue
Synagogue

Tucholskystr

Monbijoustr

Kalkscheunenstr

☆ 24

Ziegelstr

Sammlung ⊙4
Boros

Reinhardtstr

6

Luisenstr

Albrechtstr

Marienstr

Spree River
Am Weidendamm

A   **B**   Ⓤ   **C**   **D**

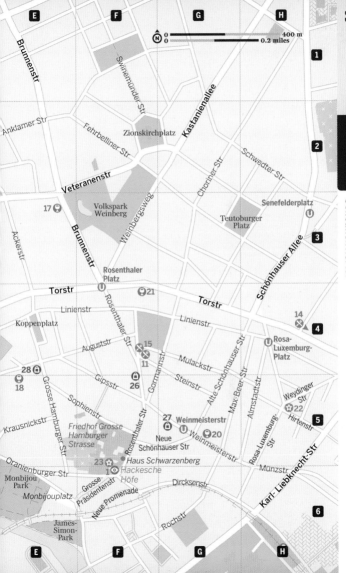

E **F** **G** **H**

0 400 m
0 0.2 miles

1

Brunnenstr

Anklamer Str

Swinemünder Str

Fehrbelliner Str

Zionskirchplatz

Kastanienallee

Choriner Str

Schwedter Str

2

Veteranenstr

17 🍴

Volkspark
Weinberg

Weinbergsweg

Teutoburger
Platz

Senefelderplatz
Ⓤ

3

Ackerstr

Brunnenstr

Schönhauser Allee

Rosenthaler
Platz
Ⓤ

Torstr

Torstr

🍴21

Linienstr

Koppenplatz

Linienstr

14
✕
4

Rosenthaler Str

Augustr

🍴15

✕
11

Mulackstr

Alte Schönhauser Str

Ⓤ Rosa-
Luxemburg-
Platz

28 🔒

18 🍴

Grosse Hamburger Str

Gipsstr

🏛
26

Gormannstr

Steinstr

Max-Beer-Str

Almstadtstr

Weydinger
Str
✮22

Hirtenstr

5

Krausnickstr

Sophienstr

Friedhof Grosse
Hamburger
Strasse

Rosenthaler Str

27
🔒

Weinmeisterstr
Ⓤ

Neue
Schönhauser Str

🍴20

Rosa-Luxemburg-Str

Oranienburger Str

23 ✮

1 🎗
Haus Schwarzenberg

Hackesche
Höfe

Dircksenstr

Münzstr

Karl-Liebknecht-Str

6

Monbijou
Park

Monbijouplatz

Grosse
Präsidentenstr

Neue Promenade

Rochstr

James-
Simon-
Park

E **F** **G** **H**

Sights

Hackesche Höfe
HISTORIC SITE

1 MAP P98, F6

The Hackesche Höfe is the largest and most famous of the courtyard ensembles peppered throughout the Scheunenviertel. Built in 1907, the eight interlinked *Höfe* reopened in 1996 with a congenial mix of cafes, galleries, shops and entertainment venues. The main entrance on Rosenthaler Strasse leads to **Court I**, prettily festooned with art nouveau tiles, while Court VII segues to the romantic **Rosenhöfe** with a sunken rose garden and tendril-like balustrades. (Hackesche Courtyards; ☏030-2809 8010; www.hackesche-hoefe.com; enter from Rosenthaler Strasse 40/41 or Sophienstrasse 6; 🚊M1, Ⓢ Hackescher Markt, Ⓤ Weinmeisterstrasse)

Hamburger Bahnhof – Museum für Gegenwart
MUSEUM

2 MAP P98, A4

Berlin's contemporary art showcase opened in 1996 in an old railway station, whose loft and grandeur are a great backdrop for this Aladdin's cave of paintings, installations, sculptures and video art. Changing exhibits span the arc of post-1950 artistic movements – from conceptual art and pop art to minimal art and Fluxus – and include works by such major players as Andy Warhol, Cy Twombly, Joseph Beuys and Robert Rauschenberg. (Contemporary Art Museum; ☏030-266 424 242; www.smb.museum; Invalidenstrasse 50-51; adult/concession €10/5, free 4-8pm 1st Thu of the month; 🕙10am-6pm Tue, Wed & Fri, to 8pm Thu, 11am-6pm Sat & Sun; 🚌M5, M8, M10, Ⓢ Hauptbahnhof, Ⓤ Hauptbahnhof)

Museum für Naturkunde
MUSEUM

3 MAP P98, A3

Fossils and minerals don't quicken your pulse? Well, how about Tristan, the T-Rex? His skeleton is among the best-preserved in the world and, along with the 12m-high *Brachiosaurus branchai,* part of the Jurassic superstar lineup at this highly engaging museum. Elsewhere you can wave at Knut, the world's most famous dead polar bear; marvel at the fragile bones of an ultrarare *Archaeopteryx* protobird, and find out why zebras are striped. (Museum of Natural History; ☏030-2093 8591; www.naturkunde museum.berlin; Invalidenstrasse 43; adult/concession incl audioguide €8/5; 🕙9.30am-6pm Tue-Fri, 10am-6pm Sat & Sun; ♿; 🚌M5, M8, M10, 12, Ⓤ Naturkundemuseum)

Sammlung Boros
GALLERY

4 MAP P98, B6

This Nazi-era bunker presents one of Berlin's finest private contemporary art collections, amassed by advertising guru Christian Boros who acquired the behemoth in 2003. A third selection of works went live in May 2017 and includes installations by Katja Novitskova, digital paintings by Avery Singer and photo series by Peter Piller. Book online (weeks, if not months, ahead) to join a guided tour (also in English) and to pick up fascinating nuggets about the building's surprising other peacetime incarnations. (Boros Collection; ☎030-2759 4065; www.sammlung-boros.de; Reinhardtstrasse 20; adult/concession €12/6; ☺tours 3-6.30pm Thu, 10.30am-6.30pm Fri, 10am-6.30pm Sat & Sun; ☒M1, ⑤Friedrichstrasse, ⓤOranienburger Tor, Friedrichstrasse)

Neue Synagoge   SYNAGOGUE

5 ◉ MAP P98, D5

The gleaming gold dome of the Neue Synagoge is the most visible symbol of Berlin's revitalised Jewish community. The 1866 original was Germany's largest synagogue but its modern incarnation is not so

much a house of worship (although prayer services do take place), as a museum and place of remembrance called **Centrum Judaicum**. The dome can be climbed from April to September (adult/concession €3/2.50). (☎030-8802 8300; www.centrumjudaicum.de; Oranienburger Strasse 28-30; adult/concession €5/4, audioguide €3; ☺10am-6pm Mon-Fri, to 7pm Sun, closes 3pm Fri & 6pm Sun Oct-Mar; ☒M1, ⓤOranienburger Tor, ⑤Oranienburger Strasse)

KW Institute for Contemporary Art   GALLERY

6 ◉ MAP P98, D4

Founded in the early 1990s in an old margarine factory, nonprofit KW played a key role in turning the Scheunenviertel into Berlin's first major post-Wall art district.

Sammlung Boros

Haus Schwarzenberg

Haus Schwarzenberg (www.haus-schwarzenberg.org; Rosenthaler Strasse 39; admission free; ⏰courtyard 24hr; 🚋M1, Ⓢ Hackescher Markt) is the last holdout in the heavily gentrified area around the Hackescher Markt. Run by a nonprofit organisation, it's an unpretentious space where art and creativity are allowed to flourish beyond the mainstream and commerce. Festooned with street art and bizarre metal sculptures, the courtyards lead to studios, offices, the underground 'amusement park' **Monsterkabinett**, the edgy-arty **Eschschloraque Rümschrümp** bar, an art-house cinema – outdoors in summer – and a couple of small **museums** dealing with Jewish persecution during the Third Reich.

It continues to stage boundary-pushing exhibits that reflect the latest – and often radical – trends in contemporary art. (📞030-243 4590; www.kw-berlin.de; Auguststrasse 69; adult/concession €8/6, free 6-9pm Thu; ⏰11am-7pm Wed-Mon, to 9pm Thu; 🚋M1, Ⓢ Oranienburger Strasse, Ⓤ Oranienburger Tor)

Berliner Medizinhistorisches Museum
MUSEUM

7 ◉ MAP P98, A4

This Charité Hospital–run museum chronicles 300 years of medical history in an anatomical theatre, a pathologist's dissection room, a laboratory and a historical patients' ward. The heart of the exhibit, though, is a sometimes grisly specimen hall whose 750 pathological-anatomical wet and dry preparations are essentially a 3D textbook on human disease and deformity. (Berlin Museum of Medical History; 📞030-450 536 156; www.bmm-charite.de; Charitéplatz 1; adult/concession €9/4; ⏰10am-5pm Tue, Thu, Fri & Sun, to 7pm Wed & Sat; 🚋M5, M10, Ⓢ Hauptbahnhof, Ⓤ Hauptbahnhof)

Eating

Katz Orange
INTERNATIONAL €€

8 ✗ MAP P98, D3

With its holistic farm-to-table menu, stylish country flair and top-notch cocktails, the 'Orange Cat' hits a gastro grand slam. It will have you purring for such perennial favourites as Duroc pork that's been slow-roasted for 12 hours (nicknamed 'candy on bone'). The setting in a castle-like former brewery is stunning, especially in summer when the patio opens. (📞030-983 208 430; www.katzorange.com; Bergstrasse 22; mains €17-24; ⏰6-11pm; 🚋M8, Ⓤ Rosenthaler Platz)

Zenkichi
JAPANESE €€€

9 ✗ MAP P98, C5

Romance runs high at this lantern-lit basement *izakaya* (Japanese pub), which serves faithfully executed gourmet Japanese fare and premium sake in cosy alcoves with black-lacquer tables shielded by bamboo blinds for extra privacy. Expect your tastebuds to do cartwheels, no matter if you treat yourself to the seasonal *omakase* (chef's) dinner or compose your own culinary symphony from the small-plate menu. (☑030-2463 0810; www.zenkichi.de; Johannisstrasse 20; 4-/8-course tasting menu €45/65, small plates €4.50-26; ☉6pm-midnight; ☑; Ⓤ Oranienburger Tor, Friedrichstrasse, Ⓢ Friedrichstrasse)

House of Small Wonder INTERNATIONAL €

10 ⓧ MAP P98, C5

A wrought-iron staircase spirals up to this brunch and lunch oasis where potted plants and whimsical decor create a relaxed backyard garden feel. The global comfort is just as beautiful, no matter if you go for eggs Benedict with home-made yoghurt scones, Okinawan Taco Rice or zoodles with cashew miso pesto. Also a good spot just for coffee and pastries. (☑030-2758 2877; www.houseofsmallwonder.de; Johannisstrasse 20; dishes €8-13; ☉9am-5pm; ☎☑; Ⓤ Oranienburger Tor, Ⓢ Oranienburger Strasse, Friedrichstrasse)

Muret La Barba ITALIAN €€

11 ⓧ MAP P98, F4

This wine shop–bar-restaurant combo exudes the kind of rustic authenticity that instantly transports *cognoscenti* to Italy. The food is hearty, inventive and made with top ingredients imported from the motherland. All wine is available by the glass or by the bottle (corkage fee €10). (☑030-2809 7212; www.muretlabarba.de; Rosenthaler Strasse 61; mains €14.50-27; ☉10am-midnight Mon-Fri, noon-midnight Sat & Sun; ☑M1, Ⓤ Rosenthaler Platz)

Schwarzwaldstuben GERMAN €€

12 ⓧ MAP P98, D4

In the mood for a Hansel and Gretel moment? Then join the other 'lost kids' for satisfying slow food from the southwest German regions of Baden and Swabia. Tuck into gut-filling platters of *spaetzle* (mac 'n' cheese), *Maultaschen* (ravioli-like pasta) or giant schnitzel with fried potatoes. Dine amid rustic and tongue-in-cheek forest decor or grab a table on the pavement. (☑030-2809 8084; www.schwarzwaldstuben-berlin.com; Tucholskystrasse 48; mains €7-16.50; ☉9am-midnight; ☑M1, Ⓢ Oranienburger Strasse)

Night Kitchen INTERNATIONAL €€

13 ⓧ MAP P98, D5

This smartly seductive courtyard bistro is often packed to capacity with punters hungry for modern Med spins inspired by the mothership in Tel Aviv. You're free to order à la carte but the guiding concept here is 'Dinner with Friends', a chef-collated meal designed for sharing. Sit inside at high tables or at the bar, or in the candlelit courtyard. (☑030-2357 5075; www.nightkitchenberlin.com; Oranienburger Strasse 32; dishes €4-19, Dinner with Friends

Stumbling Upon History

If you lower your gaze, you'll see them all over town but nowhere are they more concentrated than in the Scheunenviertel: small brass paving stones in front of house entrances. Called **Stolpersteine** (stumbling blocks), they are part of a nationwide project by Berlin-born artist Gunter Demnig and are essentially minimemorials honouring the people (usually Jews) who lived in the respective houses before being killed by the Nazis. The engravings indicate the person's name, birth year, year of deportation, the name of the concentration camp where they were taken and the date they perished.

per person €36; ⏰5pm–midnight daily, 11am-4pm Sun; 🛜📶; 🚋M1, 🅂Oranienburger Strasse, 🆄Oranienburger Tor)

Store Kitchen INTERNATIONAL €

14 ❎ MAP P98, H4

This is the kind of impossibly trendy yet welcoming place that had food fanciers in a headlock the moment it opened inside hipper-than-thou lifestyle and fashion temple the Store, on the ground floor of Soho House. Head here if you crave breakfast, salads, sandwiches and light meals that capture the latest global food trends while using local suppliers. (📞030-405 044 550; www.thestores.com; Torstrasse 1; dishes €6-12; ⏰10am-7pm Mon-Sat; 🛜; 🆄Rosa-Luxemburg-Platz)

District Môt VIETNAMESE €€

15 ❎ MAP P98, F4

At this colourful mock-Saigon street-food parlour, patrons squat on tiny plastic stools around wooden tables where rolls of toilet paper irreverently stand in for paper napkins. The small-plate menu mixes the familiar (steamy *pho* noodle soup, papaya salad) with the adventurous (stewed eel, deep-fried silk) but it's their De La Sauce *bao* burger that has collected the accolades. (📞030-2008 9284; www.districtmot.com; Rosenthaler Strasse 62; dishes €7-19; ⏰noon–midnight; 🛜; 🚋M1, 🆄Rosenthaler Platz)

Tadshikische Teestube RUSSIAN €

16 ❎ MAP P98, D5

Treat yourself to a Russian tea ceremony complete with silvery samovar, biscuits and vodka, or tuck into hearty Russian *blini* (pancakes) or *vareniki* (dumplings) while reclining amid plump pillows, hand-carved sandalwood pillars and heroic murals in this original Tajik tearoom. The authentic space was gifted by the Soviets to the East German government in 1974.

In summer the sun-dappled courtyard is a mellow spot for a bite or drink. (📞030-204 1112; www.tadshikische-teestube.de; Oranienburger Strasse 27, KunstHof; mains €7-12;

⊘4-11pm Mon-Fri, noon-11pm Sat & Sun; 🚇M1, Ⓢ Oranienburger Strasse)

Drinking

Buck & Breck   COCKTAIL BAR

17 🚇 MAP P98, E3

Liquid maestro Gonçalo de Sousa Monteiro and his baseball-cap wearing team treat grown-up patrons to libational flights of fancy in their clandestine cocktail salon with classic yet friendly flair. Historical short drinks are a strength, including the eponymous bubbly-based cocktail Buck and Breck, named for mid-19th-century US president James Buchanan and his VP John Breckinridge. (www.buckandbreck.com; Brunnenstrasse 177; ⊘7pm-late Apr-Oct, 8pm-late Nov-Mar; 🚇M1, Ⓤ Rosenthaler Platz)

Clärchens Ballhaus   CLUB

18 🚇 MAP P98, E5

Yesteryear is now at this early-20th-century dance hall where groovers and grannies hoof it across the parquet without even a touch of irony. There are different sounds nightly – salsa to swing, tango to disco – and a live band on Saturday. Dancing kicks off from 9pm or 9.30pm. Ask about dance lessons. Tables can only be reserved if you plan on eating. (📞030-282 9295; www.ballhaus.de; Auguststrasse 24; ⊘Sun-Thu free, Fri & Sat €5; ⊘11am-late; 🚇M1, Ⓢ Oranienburger Strasse)

Torbar   BAR

19 🚇 MAP P98, D4

This buzzy restaurant-bar combo owned by Dieter Meier, one half

District Môt

of the 1980s Swiss proto-techno duo Yello, is always packed with beautiful people keen on a good time and quality cocktails. Keep an eye on passers-by through the floor-to-ceiling windows or sidle up to the long bar with complexion-friendly lighting. (☏030-5520 2582; www.torbar-berlin.de; Torstrasse 183; ☺7pm-2am Wed & Thu, to 3.30am Fri & Sat; ⓤOranienburger Tor)

Father Carpenter
CAFE

20 ⭐ MAP P98, G5

Tucked into a quiet courtyard, Father Carpenter is not the kind of cafe one simply stumbles upon. Yet among coffee cognoscenti, it's very much a destination for its locally roasted Fjord java, cakes from the Albatross bakery in Kreuzberg and trendy snacks like avo toasts and vegan granola. A great refuelling stop halfway through a shopping spree. (www.fathercarpenter.com; Münzstrasse 21; ☺9am-6pm Mon-Fri, 10am-6pm Sat; ⓤWeinmeisterstrasse)

Mikkeler
CRAFT BEER

21 ⭐ MAP P98, F4

Mikkeler – the name stands for Mikkel Borg Bjergsø and Kristian Klarup Keller – dispenses craft beer that the two Danes have been brewing since 2006. In their first beer salon in Germany, their two dozen signature and guest brews on tap are best enjoyed over free-flowing conversation at the bar amid minimalist Scandinavian-woodsy surroundings. (☏0176 8314 1103; www.mikkeller.dk/location/mikkeller-berlin; Torstrasse

102; ☺3pm-midnight Sun-Thu, to 2am Fri & Sat; ⓤRosenthaler Platz)

Entertainment

Babylon
CINEMA

22 ⭐ MAP P98, H5

This top-rated indie screens a smart line-up of cinematic expression, from new German films and international art-house flicks to themed retrospectives and other stuff you'd never catch at the multiplex. For silent movies, the original theatre organ is put through its paces. Also hosts occasional readings and concerts. (☏030-242 5969; www.babylonberlin.de; Rosa-Luxemburg-Strasse 30; tickets €7-10; ⓤRosa-Luxemburg-Platz)

Chamäleon Theatre
CABARET

23 ⭐ MAP P98, F5

A marriage of art-nouveau charms and high-tech theatre trappings, this intimate venue in a 1920s-style old ballroom hosts 'contemporary circus' shows that blend comedy, acrobatics, music, juggling and dance – often in sassy, sexy and unconventional fashion. Sit at the bar, at bistro tables or in comfy armchairs. (☏030-400 0590; www.chamaeleonberlin.com; Rosenthaler Strasse 40/41; tickets €37-59; 🚋M1, Ⓢ Hackescher Markt)

Friedrichstadt-Palast Berlin
PERFORMING ARTS

24 ⭐ MAP P98, C5

Europe's largest revue theatre puts on innovative, high-tech and visually stunning shows that are an artistic amalgam of music, dance, costumes, acrobatics and stage wizardry. Most shows have a two-year run with the latest, called *Vivid,* opening in September 2018. Starring an android named R'eye, it features stunning hats by milliner-to-the-stars Philip Treacy. German language skills not required. (☎030-2326 2326; www.palast.berlin; Friedrichstrasse 107; tickets €20-130; 🚋M1, Ⓤ Oranienburger Tor, Ⓢ Friedrichstrasse, Oranienburger Strasse)

Shopping

Bonbonmacherei FOOD

25 🔒 MAP P98, D5

The aroma of peppermint and liquorice wafts through this old-fashioned basement candy kitchen whose owners use antique equipment and time-tested and modern recipes to churn out such souvenir-worthy treats as their signature leaf-shaped Berliner Maiblätter made with woodruff. Mix and match your own bag. (☎030-4405 5243; www.bonbonmacherei.de; Oranienburger Strasse 32, Heckmann Höfe; ⏰noon-7pm Wed-Sat Sep-Jun; 🚋M1, Ⓢ Oranienburger Strasse)

Kauf Dich Glücklich FASHION & ACCESSORIES

26 🔒 MAP P98, F5

What began as a waffle cafe and vintage shop has turned into a small emporium of indie concept boutiques with this branch being the flagship. It's a prettily arranged and eclectic mix of reasonably priced on-trend clothing, accessories and jewellery from the own-brand KDG-collection and other hand-picked labels, mostly from Scandinavia. (☎030-2887 8817; www.kaufdich gluecklich-shop.de; Rosenthaler Strasse 17; ⏰11am-8pm Mon-Sat; Ⓤ Weinmeisterstrasse, Rosenthaler Platz)

1. Absinth Depot Berlin FOOD & DRINKS

27 🔒 MAP P98, G5

Van Gogh, Toulouse-Lautrec and Oscar Wilde are among the fin-de-siècle artists who drew inspiration from the 'green fairy', as absinthe is also known. This quaint shop has over 100 varieties of the stuff and an expert owner who'll happily help you pick out the perfect bottle for your own mind-altering rendezvous. (☎030-281 6789; www.erstesabsinth depotberlin.de; Weinmeisterstrasse 4; ⏰2pm-midnight Mon-Fri, 1pm-midnight Sat; Ⓤ Weinmeisterstrasse)

Do You Read Me?! BOOKS

28 🔒 MAP P98, E4

Trend chasers could probably spend hours flicking through this gallery-style assortment of hip, obscure and small-print magazines from around the world. There's a distinct focus on fashion, design, architecture, music, art and contemporary trends, and knowledge-able staff to help you navigate, if needed. (☎030-6954 9695; www. doyoureadme.de; Augustsstrasse 28; ⏰10am-7.30pm Mon-Sat; Ⓢ Oranienburger Strasse, Ⓤ Rosenthaler Platz)

Explore ⊚
Kurfürstendamm & City West

The glittering heart of West Berlin during the Cold War, the famous shopping boulevard Kurfürstendamm is still among the city's biggest drawcards. Its western end, around the famous Zoo Berlin, has been undergoing major revitalisation, while nearby Schloss Charlottenburg is a treat for royal groupies. Leafy side streets, lined with palatial townhouses, still reflect the area's bourgeois charms.

Itching to shop? Get your sightseeing fix out of the way in the morning on a spin around the glorious Prussian palace of Schloss Charlottenburg (p122), then hit the boutiques lining Kurfürstendamm, pausing to ponder the futility of war at the Kaiser-Wilhelm-Gedächtniskirche (p112). Don't miss the snazzy concept mall Bikini Berlin or the grand KaDeWe (p119) department store. In the afternoon, indulge in coffee and cake at Kuchenladen (p114) before picking up redecorating ideas at Stilwerk. Celebrate dinner at Restaurant am Steinplatz (p116) or, alternatively, catch a cabaret-style show and a bite in the mirrored tent of Bar Jeder Vernunft (p118).

Getting There & Around

🚌 Zoologischer Garten is the western terminus for buses 100 and 200. M19, M29 and X10 travel along Kurfürstendamm.

Ⓢ Zoologischer Garten is the most central station and linked to Alexanderplatz by the S5 and S7.

Ⓤ Uhlandstrasse, Kurfürstendamm and Wittenbergplatz stations (U1) put you right in shopping central.

Kurfürstendamm & City West Map on p110

Kaiser-Wilhelm-Gedächtniskirche (p112) SERGEY KOHL/GETTY IMAGES ©

A

B

C

D

1

Bismarckstr

◄ ⭐ 22

26 🔒

Leibnizstr

2

Goethestr

Steinplatz

Grolmanstr

Knesebeckstr

Carmerstr

✖ 16
✖ 15

Pestalozzistr

⭐ 23

11

Uhlandstr

3

Kantstr

✖ 12

Savignyplatz

28 🔒

8 ✖

Savignyplatz

Kantstr

S 5

10

Wielandstr

Schlüterstr

Niebuhrstr

Bleibtreustr

CHARLOTTENBURG

9 ✖ 18

4

Leibnizstr

Grolmanstr

✖ 14

Mommsenstr

Knesebeckstr

Uhlandstr Ⓤ

Walter-Benjamin-
Platz

George-
Grosz-Platz

30 🔒

6
Fasanenstr

Käthe-
Kollwitz-
Museum

5

Kurfürstendamm

Bleibtreustr

Story of
Berlin

7 ◉

◄ ⭐ 24

Olivaer
Platz

Lietzenburger Str

Uhlandstr

Pariser Str

Bayerische Str

Württembergische Str

Sächsische Str

Emser Str

Pfalzburger Str

6

Fasanenplatz

Ludwigkirchplatz

Ludwigkirchstr

A

B

C

D

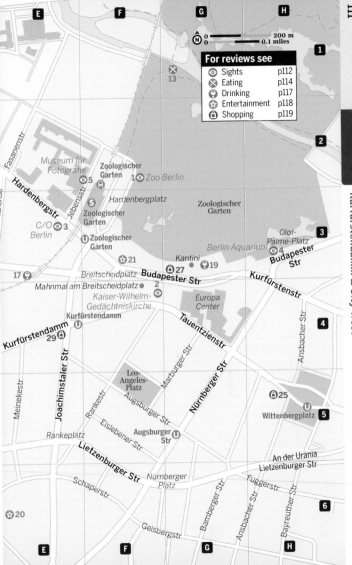

For reviews see
- ◉ Sights — p112
- ✕ Eating — p114
- 🍷 Drinking — p117
- ✪ Entertainment — p118
- 🔒 Shopping — p119

N
0 — 200 m
0 — 0.1 miles

Fasanenstr

Museum für Fotografie ◉5

Zoologischer Garten ◉1 ◉ Zoo Berlin

Hardenbergstr

Jebensstr

Hardenbergplatz

Zoologischer Garten

C/O ◉3 Berlin

Zoologischer Garten

Olof-Palme-Platz

Zoologischer Garten

Berlin Aquarium ◉4

Kantini

17 🍷

✪21

Budapester Str

Kurfürstenstr

🔒27 ✕19

Breitscheidplatz

Budapester Str

Mahnmal am Breitscheidplatz ●

Kaiser-Wilhelm-Gedächtniskirche

◉2

Europa Center

Kurfürstendamm

Kurfürstendamm Ⓤ

Tauentzienstr

29 🔒

Joachimstaler Str

Marburger Str

Nürnberger Str

Ansbacher Str

Los-Angeles-Platz

🔒25

Meinekestr

Pankestr

Augsburger Str

Wittenbergplatz Ⓤ

Eislebener Str

Augsburger Str Ⓤ

An der Urania
Lietzenburger Str

Rankeplatz

Nürnberger Platz

Lietzenburger Str

Bamberger Str

Ansbacher Str

Fuggerstr

Bayreuther Str

✪20

Schaperstr

Geisbergstr

Sights

Zoo Berlin　　ZOO

1 ◉ MAP P110, F2

Berlin's zoo holds a triple record as Germany's oldest (since 1844), most species-rich and most popular animal park. Top billing at the moment goes to a pair of bamboo-devouring pandas on loan from China. The menagerie includes nearly 20,000 critters representing 1500 species, including orangutans, koalas, rhinos, giraffes and penguins. Public feeding sessions take place throughout the day – check the schedule online and by the ticket counter. (☏030-254 010; www.zoo-berlin.de; Hardenbergplatz 8; adult/child €15.50/8, with aquarium €21/10.50; �9am-6.30pm Apr-Sep, to 6pm Mar & Oct, to 4.30pm Nov-Feb; ☐100, 200, ⑤Zoologischer Garten, ⓤZoologischer Garten, Kurfürstendamm)

Kaiser-Wilhelm-Gedächtniskirche　　CHURCH

2 ◉ MAP P110, F4

Allied bombing in 1943 left only the husk of the west tower of this once magnificent neo-Romanesque church standing. Now an antiwar memorial, it stands quiet and dignified amid the roaring traffic. Historic photographs displayed in the **Gedenkhalle** (Hall of Remembrance), at the bottom of the tower, help you visualise the former grandeur of this 1895 church. The adjacent octagonal hall of worship, added in 1961, has

glowing midnight-blue glass walls and a giant 'floating' Jesus. (Kaiser Wilhelm Memorial Church; ☏030-218 5023; www.gedaechtniskirche.com; Breitscheidplatz; admission free; ☻church 9am-7pm, memorial hall 10am-6pm Mon-Sat, noon-5.30pm Sun; ☐100, 200, ⓤZoologischer Garten, Kurfürstendamm, ⑤Zoologischer Garten)

C/O Berlin　　GALLERY

3 ◉ MAP P110, E3

Founded in 2000, C/O Berlin is the capital's most respected private, nonprofit exhibition centre for international photography and is based at the iconic Amerika Haus, which served as a United States cultural and information centre from 1957 until 2006. C/O's roster of highbrow exhibits has featured many members of the shutterbug elite, including Annie Leibovitz, Stephen Shore, Nan Goldin and Anton Corbijn. (☏030-284 441 662; www.co-berlin.org; Hardenbergstrasse 22-24; adult/concession/child under 18 €10/5/free; ☻11am-8pm; ⑤Zoologischer Garten, ⓤZoologischer Garten)

Berlin Aquarium　　AQUARIUM

4 ◉ MAP P110, H3

Three floors of exotic fish, amphibians and reptiles await at this endearingly old-fashioned aquarium with its darkened halls and glowing tanks. Some of the denizens of the famous **Crocodile Hall** could be the stuff of nightmares, but dancing jellyfish, iridescent poison frogs and a real-life 'Nemo' bring smiles to young and old. (☏030-

254 010; www.aquarium-berlin.de; Budapester Strasse 32; adult/child €15.50/8, with zoo €21/10.50; ⏰9am-6pm; 👶; ⓈZoologischer Garten, ⓊZoologischer Garten)

Museum für Fotografie MUSEUM

5 ◉ MAP P110, F2

A former Prussian officers' casino now showcases the legacy of Helmut Newton (1920–2004), the Berlin-born *enfant terrible* of fashion and lifestyle photography, with the two lower floors dedicated to his life and work. On the top floor, the gloriously restored barrel-vaulted **Kaisersaal** (Emperor's Hall) forms a grand backdrop for changing international photography exhibits. (📞030-266 424 242; www.smb.museum/mf; Jebensstrasse 2; adult/concession €10/5; ⏰11am-7pm Tue,

Wed & Fri-Sun, to 8pm Thu; ⓈZoologischer Garten, ⓊZoologischer Garten)

Käthe-Kollwitz-Museum MUSEUM

6 ◉ MAP P110, D5

Käthe Kollwitz (1867–1945) was a famous early-20th-century artist whose social and political awareness lent a tortured power to her lithographs, graphics, woodcuts, sculptures and drawings. This four-floor exhibit in a charming 19th-century villa kicks off with an introduction to this extraordinary woman, who lived in Berlin for 52 years, before presenting a life-spanning selection of her work, including the powerful anti-hunger lithography *Brot!* (Bread!, 1924) and the woodcut series *Krieg* (War,

Elephant Gate, Zoo Berlin

1922–23). (☏030-882 5210; www.
kaethe-kollwitz.de; Fasanenstrasse 24;
adult/concession/child under 18 €7/4/
free, audioguide €3; ⏰11am-6pm;
Ⓤ Uhlandstrasse)

Story of Berlin

MUSEUM

7 ◉ MAP P110, C5

This engaging museum breaks 800
years of Berlin history into bite-size
chunks that are easy to swallow but
substantial enough to be satisfying. Each of the 23 rooms uses
sound, light, technology and original
objects to zero in on a specific
theme or epoch in the city's history,
from its founding in 1237 to the fall
of the Berlin Wall. Tickets include
a 45-minute tour (in English) of
a still-functional 1970s atomic
bomb shelter beneath the building.
(☏030-8872 0100; www.story-of-berlin.
de; Kurfürstendamm 207-208, enter via
Ku'damm Karree mall; adult/concession/
child €12/9/5; ⏰10am-8pm, last admission 6pm; 🚌X9, X10, 109, 110, M19,
M29, TXL, Ⓤ Uhlandstrasse)

Eating

Kuchenladen

CAFE €

8 ❌ MAP P110, B3

Even size-0 locals can't resist the
siren call of this classic cafe whose
homemade cakes are like works of
art wrought from flour, sugar and
cream. From cheesecake to carrot
cake to the ridiculously rich Sach-
er Torte, it's all delicious down to
the last crumb. (☏030-3101 8424;
www.derkuchenladen.de; Kantstrasse
138; cakes €2.50-4.50; ⏰10am-8pm;
Ⓢ Savignyplatz)

Koshary Lux

MIDDLE EASTERN €

9 ❌ MAP P110, C4

This darling snack shack deals
in contemporary riffs on North
African and Middle Eastern street-
food staples. Positively addictive
is the namesake *koshary*, a rich
mix of lentils, macaroni and rice
served with caramelised onions,
chickpeas, tomato sauce and
a pistachio-spice blend. It goes
well with a homemade mint-lime
lemonade. Skip the lunch rush.
(☏030-8140 6190; www.klx-koshary
lux.com; Grolmanstrasse 27; mains
€4.50-9.20; ⏰noon-3pm & 6-9pm
Mon-Thu, noon-10pm Fri & Sat; Ⓢ Savignyplatz, Ⓤ Uhlandstrasse)

Butcher

BURGERS €€

10 ❌ MAP P110, C3

With its bar and DJ line-up,
Butcher injects a dose of hip into
the 'hood. It also knows how to
build one hell of a burger. Prime
ingredients, including Aberdeen
Angus beef, house-baked buns
and a secret sauce, make their
patty-and-bun combos shine. Rib
lovers *must* try the baby back ribs,
slow-cooked to perfection. (☏030-
323 015 673; www.the-butcher.com;
Kantstrasse 144; burgers €9.50-12.50;
⏰7am-midnight Sun-Thu, to 2am Fri &
Sat; 🛜; Ⓢ Savignyplatz)

Dicke Wirtin

GERMAN €€

11 ❌ MAP P110, C3

Old Berlin charm is in every nook
and cranny of this been-here-
forever pub, which pours eight

Berlin in the 'Golden' Twenties

The 1920s began as anything but golden, marked by a lost war, social and political instability, hyperinflation, hunger and disease. Many Berliners responded by behaving like there was no tomorrow and made their city as much a den of decadence as a cauldron of creativity. Cabaret, Dada and jazz flourished. Pleasure pits popped up everywhere, turning the city into a 'sextropolis' of Dionysian dimensions. Bursting with energy, it became a laboratory for anything new and modern, drawing giants of architecture (Hans Scharoun, Walter Gropius), fine arts (George Grosz, Max Beckmann) and literature (Bertolt Brecht, Christopher Isherwood).

Cafes & Cabaret

Cabarets provided a titillating fantasy of play and display where singers, magicians, dancers and other entertainers made audiences forget the harsh realities. Kurfürstendamm evolved into a major nightlife hub with glamorous cinemas, theatres and restaurants. The Romanisches Café, on the site of today's Europa-Center, was practically the second living room for artists, actors, writers, photographers, film producers and other creative types, some famous, most not. German writer Erich Kästner even called it the 'waiting room of the talented'.

Celluloid History

The 1920s and early '30s were also a boom time for Berlin cinema, with Marlene Dietrich seducing the world and the mighty UFA studio producing virtually all of Germany's celluloid output. Fritz Lang, whose seminal works *Metropolis* (1926) and *M* (1931) brought him international fame, was among the dominant filmmakers.

The Crash

The fun came to an instant end when the US stock market crashed in 1929, plunging the world into economic depression. Within weeks, half a million Berliners were jobless, and riots and demonstrations again ruled the streets. The volatile, increasingly polarised political climate led to clashes between communists and the emerging NS-DAP (Nazi Party), led by Adolf Hitler. Soon jackboots, Brownshirts, oppression and fear would dominate daily life in Germany.

draught beers (including the superb Kloster Andechs) and nearly three dozen homemade schnapps varieties. Hearty local and German fare, such as meatballs in caper sauce, beef liver and pork roast, keeps brains balanced. Bargain lunches, too. (☏030-312 4952; www.

Mahnmal am Breitscheidplatz

This simple **memorial** (Map p110, F4; Breitscheidplatz; 🚌100, 200, Ⓤ Zoologischer Garten, Ⓢ Zoologischer Garten) honours the victims of the terror attack of 19 December 2016, when an Islamist asylum seeker drove into a crowd at the Christmas market held every year on Breitscheidplatz. Unveiled on the event's one-year anniversary, it consists of a golden crack that runs down the steps descending from the Kaiser Wilhelm Memorial Church, with the names of the dozen victims chiselled into the front of the steps.

dicke-wirtin.de; Carmerstrasse 9; mains €11-18; ⏱11am-late; Ⓢ Savignyplatz)

Good Friends   CHINESE €€

12 🍴 MAP P110, B3

Good Friends is widely considered Berlin's best Cantonese restaurant. The ducks in the window are merely an overture to a menu long enough to confuse Confucius, including plenty of authentic homestyle dishes (on a separate menu). If steamed chicken feet prove too challenging, you can always fall back on sweet-and-sour pork or fried rice with shrimp. (📞030-313 2659; www.goodfriends-berlin.de; Kantstrasse 30; 2-course weekday lunch €7-7.70, dinner mains €8-21; ⏱noon-1am; Ⓢ Savignyplatz)

Schleusenkrug   GERMAN €€

13 🍴 MAP P110, G1

Sitting pretty on the edge of the Tiergarten park, next to a canal lock, Schleusenkrug truly comes into its own during beer-garden season. People from all walks of life hunker over big mugs and comfort food – from grilled sausages to *Flammkuchen* (Alsatian pizza) and weekly specials. Breakfast is served until 2pm. (📞030-313 9909; www.schleusenkrug.de; Müller-Breslau-Strasse; mains €6-16; ⏱10am-midnight May-Sep, 11am-6pm Oct-Apr; Ⓢ Zoologischer Garten, Ⓤ Zoologischer Garten)

Schwein   INTERNATIONAL €€€

14 🍴 MAP P110, B4

This casual fine-dining lair delivers the perfect trifecta – fabulous food, wine and long drinks. Order the multicourse menu to truly experience the genius of kitchen champion Christopher Kümper, who creates globally inspired and regionally sourced symphonies of taste and textures. Or keep it 'casual' with just a bite and a gin and tonic. (📞030-2435 6282; www.schwein.online; Mommsenstrasse 63; dishes €13-37, 4-/5-course menu €65/75; ⏱6pm-midnight Mon-Fri, to 2am Sat; 🛜📷; Ⓢ Savignyplatz)

Restaurant am Steinplatz   GERMAN €€€

15 🍴 MAP P110, D2

The 1920s get a 21st-century make-over at this stylish outpost with an open kitchen, where chef Nicholas

Hahn and team create dishes with technique and passion. The menu takes diners on a culinary romp around Germany with occasional touchdowns in other countries, resulting in intellectually ambitious but super-satisfying dishes that often star unusual or rare ingredients. (☎030-554 444, ext 7053; www.hotelsteinplatz.com; Steinplatz 4; 2-/3-course lunch €19/23, dinner mains €23-30; ⏰noon-2.30pm & 6-10pm Mon-Fri, 6-10pm Sat & Sun; P; 🚌M45, U Ernst-Reuter-Platz, Zoologischer Garten, S Zoologischer Garten)

Drinking

Bar am Steinplatz COCKTAIL BAR

16 MAP P110, D2

Christian Gentemann's liquid playground at the art-deco **Hotel am Steinplatz** was crowned 'hotel bar of the year' in 2016 and 2017, and for good reason The drinks are simply sensational and the ambience a perfect blend of hip and grown-up. The illustrated cocktail menu teases the imagination by listing ingredients and tastes for each drink instead of just an abstract name. (☎030-554 4440; www.hotelsteinplatz.com; Steinplatz 4; ⏰4pm-late; U Ernst-Reuter-Platz)

Bar Zentral COCKTAIL BAR

17 MAP P110, E3

A top libation station, Zentral is run by two local bar gurus who offer up a seriously crafted palette of classics and new-falutin' potions, amid decor that defines elegant understatement. Instead of glowing in a well-lit backbar, bottles

Monkey Bar (p118)

Elevated Fast Food at Kantini 🍽

Kantini (Map p110, G3; Budapester Strasse, Bikini Berlin; ⏱10am-8pm Mon-Sat; 🍴🚼; Ⓤ Zoologischer Garten, Ⓢ Zoologischer Garten) is a next-gen food court at the stylish Bikini Berlin shopping mall. It sports Instaworthy looks thanks to its mash-up of industrial edge and playful design touches, including potted plants, candy-coloured furniture and Berlin Zoo views. The 13 eateries pick up on tradition and trends – from Berlin *Currywurst* to Hawaiian poké bowls – often with high quality.

discreetly hide in black cabinets that form a nice contrast to the long wooden bar. (📞030-3743 3079; www.barzentral.de; Lotte-Lenya-Bogen 551; ⏱5pm-late; Ⓢ Zoologischer Garten, Ⓤ Zoologischer Garten, Kurfürstendamm)

Diener Tattersall   PUB

18 🍺 MAP P110, C4

In business for over a century, this Old Berlin haunt was taken over by German heavyweight champion Franz Diener in the 1950s and became one of West Berlin's iconic artist pubs. From Billy Wilder to Harry Belafonte, they all came for beer and *Bulette* (meat patties) and left behind signed black-and-white photographs that grace Diener's walls to this day.

(📞030-881 5329; www.diener-berlin. de; Grolmanstrasse 47; ⏱6pm-2am; Ⓢ Savignyplatz)

Monkey Bar   BAR

19 🍸 MAP P110, G3

On the 10th floor of the **25hours Hotel Bikini Berlin**, this mainstream-hip 'urban jungle' delivers fabulous views of the city and Zoo Berlin while the menu gives prominent nods to tiki concoctions (great Mai Tai!) and gin-based cocktail sorcery. Come early for chilled sundowners on the sweeping terrace. Different DJs spin nightly Friday to Sunday, from 4pm. (📞030-120 221 210; www.monkeybarberlin.de; Budapester Strasse 40; ⏱noon-2am; 🛜; 🚌100, 200, Ⓢ Zoologischer Garten, Ⓤ Zoologischer Garten)

Entertainment

Bar Jeder Vernunft   CABARET

20 ⭐ MAP P110, E6

Life's still a cabaret at this intimate 1912 mirrored art-nouveau tent theatre, one of Berlin's most beloved venues for sophisticated song-and-dance shows, comedy and *chansons* (songs). Sip a glass of bubbly while relaxing at a candlelit cafe table or in a curvy red-velvet booth bathed in flickering candlelight reflected in the mirrors. Many shows don't require German-language skills. (📞030-883 1582; www.bar-jeder-vernunft.de; Schaperstrasse 24; admission varies; Ⓤ Spichernstrasse)

Zoo Palast   CINEMA

21 ⭐ MAP P110, F3

Old-school glamour meets state-of-the-art technology and comfort at this rejuvenated grand cinema, which saw international stars sashay over the red carpet during the Berlinale film fest between 1957 and 1999. It screens mostly 2D and 3D blockbusters (dubbed into German) in seven fancily appointed theatres. Check out the cool 1950s foyer. (📞030-254 010; www.zoopalast-berlin.de; Hardenbergstrasse 29a; tickets €9-19; 🚌100, 200, Ⓢ Zoologischer Garten, Ⓤ Zoologischer Garten)

Deutsche Oper Berlin   OPERA

22 ⭐ MAP P110, A1

Founded by Berliners in 1912 as a counterpoint to the royal opera on Unter den Linden, the Deutsche Oper presents a classic 19th-century opera repertory from Verdi and Puccini to Wager and Strauss, all sung in their original languages. If you like your opera more experimental, check out the Tischlerei (joinery), a studio space for boundary-pushing (and more budget-friendly) musical interpretations. (German Opera Berlin; 📞030-3438 4343; www.deutscheoperberlin.de; Bismarckstrasse 35; tickets €22-128; Ⓤ Deutsche Oper)

A-Trane   JAZZ

23 ⭐ MAP P110, C3

Herbie Hancock and Diana Krall have graced the stage of this intimate jazz club, but mostly it's emerging talent bringing their A-game to the A-Trane. Entry is free on Monday, when local boy Andreas Schmidt and his band get everyone toe-tapping, and after midnight on Saturday for the late-night jam session. Concerts start at 9pm. (📞030-313 2550; www.a-trane.de; Bleibtreustrasse 1; admission varies; ⏰8pm-1am Sun-Thu, to late Fri & Sat; Ⓢ Savignyplatz)

Schaubühne   THEATRE

24 ⭐ MAP P110, A5

In a converted 1920s expressionist cinema by Erich Mendelsohn, Schaubühne is western Berlin's main stage for experimental, contemporary theatre, usually with a critical and analytical look at current social and political issues. The ensemble is directed by Thomas Ostermeier and includes many top names from German film and TV. Some performances feature English or French surtitles. (📞030-890 023; www.schaubuehne.de; Kurfürstendamm 153; tickets €7-48; Ⓤ Adenauerplatz)

Shopping

KaDeWe   DEPARTMENT STORE

25 🔒 MAP P110, H5

Continental Europe's largest department store has been going strong since 1907 and boasts an assortment so vast that a pirate-style campaign is the best way to plunder its bounty. If pushed for time, at least hurry up to the legendary 6th-floor gourmet food hall. The name, by the way, stands for *Kaufhaus des Westens* (department store of the West). (📞030-212 10; www.kadewe.de; Tauentzienstrasse 21-24; 🕐10am-8pm Mon-Thu, to 9pm Fri, 9.30am-8pm Sat; Ⓤ Wittenbergplatz)

Manufactum   HOMEWARES

26 🅐 MAP P110, C1

Long before sustainable became a buzzword, this shop (the brainchild of a German Green Party member) stocked traditionally made quality products from around the world, many of which have stood the test of time. Cool finds include hand-forged iron pans by Turk, lavender soap from

a French monastery and Japanese knives by Kenyo. (📞030-2403 3844; www.manufactum.de; Hardenbergstrasse 4-5; 🕐10am-8pm Mon-Fri, to 6pm Sat; Ⓤ Ernst-Reuter-Platz)

Bikini Berlin   MALL

27 🅐 MAP P110, G3

Germany's first concept mall opened in 2014 in a smoothly rehabilitated 1950s architectural icon nicknamed 'Bikini' because of its design: 200m-long upper and lower sections separated by an open floor, now chastely covered by a glass facade. Inside are three floors of urban indie boutiques, short-lease pop-up 'boxes' for up-and-comers, and an international street-food court. (📞030-5549 6455; www.bikiniberlin.de; Budapester Strasse 38-50; 🕐shops 10am-8pm Mon-Sat, Bldg 9am-8.30pm Mon-Sat, noon-6pm Sun; 🚇; 🚌100, 200, Ⓤ Zoologischer Garten, Ⓢ Zoologischer Garten)

Stilwerk   HOMEWARES

28 🅐 MAP P110, D3

This four-storey temple of good taste will have devotees of the finer things itching to redecorate. Everything you could possibly want for home and hearth is here – from key rings to grand pianos and vintage lamps – representing over 500 brands in 55 stores. (📞030-315 150; www.stilwerk.de/berlin; Kantstrasse 17; 🕐10am-7pm Mon-Sat; Ⓢ Savignyplatz)

Shopping Primer

Kurfürstendamm and Tauentzienstrasse are chock-a-block with outlets of international chains flogging fashion and accessories. Further west on Ku'damm are the more high-end boutiques such as Hermès, Cartier and Bulgari. Kantstrasse is the go-to zone for home designs. Connecting side streets, such as Bleibtreustrasse and Schlüterstrasse, house upscale indie and designer boutiques, bookshops and galleries, while Bikini Berlin features cutting-edge concept and flagship stores.

KaDeWe (p119)

Käthe Wohlfahrt ARTS & CRAFTS

🟢 29 🏠 MAP P110, E4

With its mind-boggling assortment of traditional German Yuletide decorations and ornaments, this shop lets you celebrate Christmas year-round. It's accessed via a ramp that spirals around an 8m-high ornament-laden Christmas tree. (📞09861-4090; www.wohlfahrt. com; Kurfürstendamm 225-226; 🕑10am-6pm Mon-Fri, to 6.30pm Sat; Ⓤ Kurfürstendamm)

Hautnah FASHION & ACCESSORIES

🟢 30 🏠 MAP P110, D5

Given the sort of city Berlin is, sooner or later you may just need to update your fetish wardrobe, and Hautnah's three floors of erotic outfits should do the job naughtily. Expect a vast range of latex bodices, leather goods, themed get-ups, sex toys and vertiginous footwear, plus wine and bubbly in the Marquis de Sade cellar. (📞030-882 3434; www.hautnahberlin.de; Uhlandstrasse 170; 🕑noon-7pm Mon-Fri, to 4pm Sat; Ⓤ Uhlandstrasse)

Worth a Trip 👀
Schloss Charlottenburg

*Schloss Charlottenburg is an exquisite baroque
palace and the best place in Berlin to soak up the
one-time grandeur of the royal Hohenzollern clan.
A visit is especially pleasant in summer, when you
can fold a stroll around the palace garden into
a day of peeking at royal treasures and lavishly
furnished period rooms reflecting centuries of
royal tastes and lifestyles.*

📞 030-320 910

www.spsg.de

Spandauer Damm 10-22

day pass to all 4 bldgs
adult/concession €17/13

🕑 hours vary by bldg

🚌 M45, 109, 309,
Ⓤ Richard-Wagner-Platz,
Sophie-Charlotte-Platz

Altes Schloss

The central Old Palace is fronted by Andreas Schlüter's grand **equestrian statue of the Great Elector** (1699). Inside, the baroque living quarters of Friedrich I and Sophie-Charlotte are an extravaganza in stucco, brocade and overall opulence. Highlights include the **Oak Gallery**, the charming **Oval Hall** overlooking the park, Friedrich I's bedchamber and the **Eosander Chapel** with its trompe l'œil arches. The king's passion for precious china is reflected in the dazzling Porcelain Chamber, which is smothered in nearly 3000 pieces of Chinese and Japanese blue ware.

Neuer Flügel

The palace's most beautiful rooms are the flamboyant private quarters of Frederick the Great in the **new wing** (adult/concession incl audio guide €10/7; ⏱10am-5.30pm Tue-Sun Apr-Oct, to 5pm Tue-Sun Nov & Dec, to 4.30pm Tue-Sun Jan-Mar; 🚌M45, 109, 309) extension, designed in 1746 by royal buddy and star architect of the period Georg Wenzeslaus von Knobelsdorff. The confection-like **White Hall** banquet room and the **Golden Gallery**, a rococo fantasy of mirrors and gilding, are both standouts. Fans of 18th-century French masters such as Watteau and Pesne will also get an eyeful. Frederick the Great's nephew and successor added a summer residence with Chinese and Etruscan design elements as well as the more sombre **Winter Chambers** where a bedroom designed by Schinkel for Queen Luise is a standout.

Schlossgarten

The expansive palace park is part formal French, part unruly English and all picturesque playground. Hidden among the shady paths, flower beds, lawns, mature trees and carp pond are two smaller royal buildings, the sombre Mausoleum and the dainty Belvedere.

★ **Top Tips**

○ The 'charlotten-burg+' ticket (adult/concession €17/13) is a day pass valid for one-day admission to every open building.

○ Skip the queue by buying timed tickets at http://tickets.spsg.de (€2 service fee).

○ A palace visit is easily combined with a spin around the trio of adjacent art museums.

🍴 **Take a Break**

Enjoy a hearty German meal and a cold beer at **Brauhaus Lemke** (☎030-3087 8979; www.lemke.berlin; Luisenplatz 1; mains €12-22; ⏱noon-midnight; 🚌M45, 109, 309, Ⓤrichard-Wagner-Platz), a short walk from the palace.

★ **Getting There**

Schloss Charlottenburg is is 3km north-west of Zoologischer Garten.

Ⓤ U7 to Richard-Wagner-Platz or U2 to Sophie-Charlotte-Platz, then 1km walk.

🚌 M45 and 109 to Luisenplatz/Schloss Charlottenburg stop, or 309 to Schoss Charlottenburg stop.

Belvedere

The late-rococo **Belvedere** (adult/concession €4/3; ⏱10am-5.30pm Tue-Sun Apr-Oct) palace, with its distinctive cupola, got its start in 1788 as a private sanctuary for Friedrich Wilhelm II. These days it houses **porcelain** masterpieces by the royal manufacturer KPM, which was established in 1763 by Frederick the Great.

Neuer Pavilion

This Karl Friedrich Schinkel-designed **mini-palace** (New Pavilion; adult/concession €4/3; ⏱10am-5.30pm Tue-Sun Apr-Oct, noon-4pm Tue-Sun Nov-Mar) was a summer retreat modelled on neoclassical Italian villas. Today, it presents **paintings and sculpture** from the Biedermeier and Romantic periods.

Mausoleum

The 1810 temple-shaped **Mausoleum** (€3; ⏱10am-5.30pm Tue-Sun Apr-Oct) was conceived as the final resting place of Queen Luise, and was twice expanded to make room for other royals,. Their **marble sarcophagi** are exquisitely sculpted works of art.

Nearby: Museum Berggruen

Picasso is especially well represented with paintings, drawings and sculptures from all major creative phases at this delightful **museum** (☎030-266 424 242; www.smb.museum/mb; Schlossstrasse 1; adult/concession incl Sammlung Scharf-Gerstenberg €10/5; ⏱10am-6pm Tue-Fri, from 11am Sat & Sun; P). Elsewhere it's off to Paul Klee's emotional world, Matisse's paper cut-outs, Giacometti's famous sculptures and a sprinkling of African art that inspired them all .

Nearby: Sammlung Scharf-Gerstenberg

This stellar **collection** (☎030-266 424 242; www.smb.museum; Schlossstrasse 70; adult/concession incl Museum Berggruen €10/5; ⏱10am-6pm Tue-Fri, from 11am Sat & Sun) showcases 250 years of surrealist art, including large bodies of work by René Magritte and Max Ernst. Standouts among their 18th-century forerunners include Goya's spooky etchings and the creepy dungeon scenes by Italian engraver Giovanni Battista Piranesi. Post-WWII surrealist interpretations are represented by Jean Dubuffet.

Nearby: Bröhan Museum

This fine **museum** (☎030-3269 0600; www.broehan-museum.de; Schlossstrasse 1a; adult/concession/child under 18 €8/5/free; ⏱10am-6pm Tue-Sun) trains the spotlight on applied arts from the late 19th century until the outbreak of WWII. Pride of place goes to the **art nouveau collection**, with period rooms, furniture, porcelain and glass art from England, France, Germany, Scandinavia and Austria. A picture gallery with works by Berlin Secession artists complements the exhibits.

SCHLOSS CHARLOTTENBURG

0   200 m
0   0.1 miles

Olbersstr

Brahestr

Kamminer Str

Tegeler Weg

Osnabrücker Str

Belvedere

Schlossgarten
Charlottenburg

Spree River

Carp
Pond

Mausoleum

Schlossbrücke
boat landing
docks

Schlossgarten

Neuer
Pavillon

Tour Boat Landing
Schlossbrücke
Charlottenburg

Altes
Schloss

Neuer Flügel

Schloss
Charlottenburg

Brauhaus
Lemke

Kleine
Orangerie

Spandauer Damm

Museum
Berggruen

Sammlung
Scharf-
Gerstenberg

Schlossstr

Bröhan
Museum

Walking Tour 🚶

A Saunter Through Schöneberg

Schöneberg flaunts a mellow middle-class identity but has a radical pedigree rooted in the '80s. Its multifaceted character unfolds as you stroll from bourgeois Viktoria-Luise-Platz through Berlin's original gay quarter and along streets packed tight with boho cafes and smartly curated indie boutiques, to wind up at ethnically flavoured Hauptstrasse where David Bowie bunked back in the 1970s.

Getting There

Schöneberg is wedged between Kurfürstendamm and Kreuzberg.

Ⓤ This itinerary is bookended by two stations: Viktoria- Luise-Platz (U4) and Kleistpark (U7).

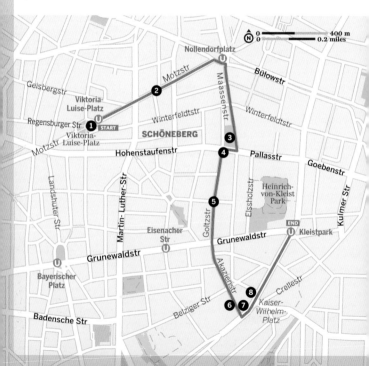

❶ Viktoria-Luise-Platz

Schöneberg's prettiest **square** is a symphony of flower beds, old trees, a lusty fountain and benches where locals swap gossip or watch kids at play. It's framed by cafes and 19th-century townhouses; note the ornate facades at Nos 7, 12 and 12a.

❷ Nollendorfplatz & the 'Gay Village'

Nollendorfplatz has been the gateway to Berlin's historic **gay quarter** since the 1920s, when Christopher Isherwood penned Berlin Stories (which inspired Cabaret) while living at Nollendorfstrasse 17. Rainbow flags still fly proudly above bars and businesses, especially along Motzstrasse and Fuggerstrasse. A memorial plaque at the U-Bahn station commemorates Nazi-era LGBT victims.

❸ Farmers Market

If it's Wednesday or Saturday morning, you're in luck because ho-hum **Winterfeldtplatz** erupts with farm-fresh fare. Along with seasonal produce you'll find handmade cheeses, cured meats, olives, local honey and plenty more staples and surprises. Saturday also has artsy-craftsy stalls.

❹ Chocophile Alert

Winterfeldt Schokoladen
(☎030-2362 3256; www.winterfeldt-schokoladen.de; Goltzstrasse 23; ⏱9am-8pm Mon-Fri, to 6pm Sat, noon-7pm Sun; Ⓤ Nollendorfplatz) stocks a vast range of international handmade gourmet chocolates, all displayed gallery-style in the original oak fixtures of a 19th-century pharmacy that doubles as a cafe.

❺ Boutique-Hopping

Goltzstrasse and its extension **Akazienstrasse** teem with indie boutiques selling vintage threads, slinky underwear and handmade jewellery, exotic teas and cooking supplies. No high-street chain in sight.

❻ Double Eye

Javaholics cherish the award-winning espresso of **Double Eye** (☎0179 456 6960; Akazienstrasse 22; ⏱8.30am-6.30pm Mon-Fri, 9am-6pm Sat; Ⓤ Eisenacher Strasse), which is why no one minds the inevitable queue.

❼ Möve im Felsenkeller

An artist hang-out since the 1920s, this cosy **pub** (☎030-781 3447; Akazienstrasse 2; ⏱4pm-midnight Mon-Sat; Ⓤ Eisenacher Strasse) was where Jeffrey Eugenides penned his 2002 Pulitzer Prize–winning novel, Middlesex. A stuffed seagull dangling from the ceiling keeps an eye on patrons seeking inspiration from eight beers on tap.

❽ Hauptstrasse

The Turkish supermarket **Öz-Gida** (☎030-7871 5291; www.ozgida.de; Hauptstrasse 16; ⏱8am-8pm Mon-Sat; Ⓤ Kleistpark) is known citywide for its olive selection, cheese spreads and quality meats. David Bowie and Iggy Pop shared a pad at Hauptstrasse 155.

Explore ◈

Kreuzberg & Neukölln

Eastern Kreuzberg and northern Neukölln across the Landwehrkanal are the epicentres of free-wheeling, multicultural and alternative Berlin. Come here to track down fabulous street art, scarf a doner kebab, browse vintage stores and hang by the canal, then find out why the area is also known as the ultimate night-crawler's paradise.

Kreuzberg sleeps late so don't come down until midday when shops and cafes finally kick into gear. Fuel up at Burgermeister (p138), then forage for vintage along Oranienstrasse and Skalitzer Strasse while keeping an eye out for fabulous street art (p138). If the sun's out, build a swim-and-tan break at Badeschiff (p136) into your day before heading down to Tempelhofer Feld (p93) for a wacky round of minigolf. Catch sunset with a view at Klunkerkranich (p133), then dedicate the rest of the night to a bar hop along Weserstrasse or around Kottbusser Tor (or both), perhaps grabbing a doner kebab for balance.

Getting There & Around

🚌 M29 links Potsdamer Platz with Oranienstrasse via Checkpoint Charlie; the M41 (also coming from Potsdamer Platz) travels through the Bergmannkiez to Neukölln via Hermannplatz.

Ⓤ Kottbusser Tor (U8) puts you into the thick of things. For Neukölln, Schönleinstrasse, Hermannplatz and Boddin-strasse (all on the U8) as well as Rathaus Neukölln (U7) are key stops.

Kreuzberg & Neukölln Map on p134

Kreuzberg & Neukölln Map on p134

Burgermeister (p138) TRAVELSTOCK44/ALAMY STOCK PHOTO ©

Walking Tour 🥾

Kotti Bar Hop

Noisy, chaotic and sleepless, the area around Kottbusser Tor U-Bahn station (Kotti, for short) defiantly retains the punky-funky alt feel that's defined it since the 1970s. Definitely more gritty than pretty, this beehive of snack shops, cafes, pubs and bars is a launchpad into some of the city's most hot-stepping nighttime action and is tailor-made for dedicated barhopping.

Walk Facts

Start Kottbusser Tor,
Ⓤ Kottbusser Tor

End Oranienstrasse,
Ⓤ Kottbusser Tor

Length 1.5km; one to six hours

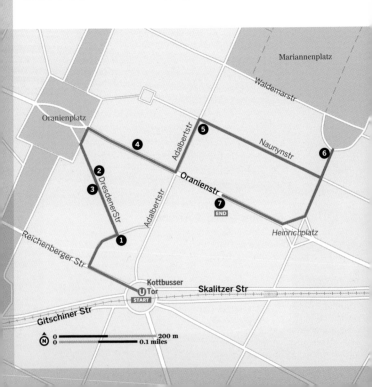

❶ Funky Salon

Tucked behind a pile of Turkish kebab shops, grocers and shisha bars, **Möbel Olfe** (📞 030-2327 4690; www.moebel-olfe.de; Reichenberger Strasse 177; ⏱6pm-3am or later Tue-Sun; Ⓤ Kottbusser Tor) is a queer-leaning drinking saloon that channels the area's alternative vibe with boho decor, strong Polish beers and a chatty vibe.

❷ Grape Delights

Great for earlier in the evening, **Otto Rink** (www.ottorink.de; Dresdener Strasse 124; ⏱6pm-2am; Ⓤ Kottbusser Tor) is an easy-going place to discover just how wonderful German wines can be. There's an emphasis on white varietals from the Moselle region, but wines from other German areas also feature on the menu.

❸ 1950s Cocktail Cave

If it's transcendent cocktails you're lusting after, point the compass to **Würgeengel** (📞 030-615 5560; www.wuergeengel.de; Dresdener Strasse 122; ⏱7pm-2am or later; Ⓤ Kottbusser Tor), a stylish art-decostyle bar with chandeliers and shiny black surfaces. The name pays homage to the surreal 1962 Buñuel movie Exterminating Angel.

❹ Luscious Lair

A fixture on Kreuzberg's hipster circuit, the vintage decor at **Luzia** (📞 030-8179 9958; www.facebook.com/luziabar; Oranienstrasse 34; ⏱noon-5am; Ⓤ Kottbusser Tor) gets updated with a mural by street artist Chin

Chin. It's a comfy spot with lighting that gives even pasty-faced hipsters a glow. There's a smokers' lounge.

❺ Gateway to Hell

Popular with punks and alternative types, the **Trinkteufel** (Drink Devil; 📞 030-614 7128; www.facebook.com/TrinkteufelKreuzberg; Naunynstrasse 60; ⏱2pm-4am Sun-Thu, to 10 am Fri & Sat; Ⓤ Kottbusser Tor) is the dive bar where Pete Doherty downed a few before getting briefly arrested in 2009 after smashing a car window. Ponder this as you hang out by the bar and check out the trippy decor while swilling a cold brew.

❻ Easy Medicine

Whatever ails you may well be fixed after dropping by the **Apotheken Bar** (📞 030-6951 8108; www.facebook.com/apothekenbar; Mariannenplatz 6; ⏱6pm-1am Mon, to 2am Tue-Thu, to 4am Fri & Sat, 5pm-midnight Sun; Ⓤ Kottbusser Tor) a vintage outpost in a 19th- century pharmacy. The fixtures and old objects like a scale, bottles and signs form the atmospheric setting for expert cocktails, some featuring homemade tonic water and other potions.

❼ Camp of Glam

A mashup of trash, camp and fun, **Roses** (📞 030-615 6570; Oranienstrasse 187; ⏱10pm-6am; Ⓤ Kottbusser Tor) is a beloved pit stop for queers and their friends. Don't let the furry walls and a predominance of pink distract you from the fact that this place takes drinking seriously until the early morning hours.

Walking Tour 🥾

Nosing Around Neukölln

Northern Neukölln knows what it's like to go from troubled neighbourhood to hipster haven. For decades the area made headlines, mostly for its high crime rate and poor schools, only to get 'discovered' a few years ago by a cash-poor and idea-rich international crowd. Today the 'hood flaunts a thriving DIY ethos and teems with funky bars, galleries, project spaces and cafes, most of them run by a cast of creative neo-Berliners.

Walk Facts

Start Maybachufer;
U Schönleinstrasse

End Neuköllner Arcaden;
U Rathaus Neukölln

Length 3km; one to two hours without stops

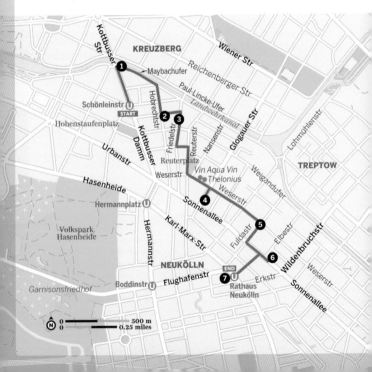

❶ Canalside Marketeering

Start by walking along the May-bachufer, a scenic section of the Landwehrkanal, ideally on Tuesday or Friday afternoons when the **Türkischer Markt** (Turkish Market; www.tuerkenmarkt.de; Maybachufer; ⏱11am-6.30pm Tue & Fri; Ⓤ Schönleinstrasse) is in full swing. Join hipsters in their quest for exotic cheese spreads, crusty flatbreads and mountains of produce.

❷ Vintage & Coffee

Is it a store? Or a cafe? In fact, **Sing Blackbird** (📞030-5484 5051; www.facebook.com/singblackbird; Sanderstrasse 11; ⏱1.30-7.30pm Mon-Sat; 📶; Ⓤ Schönleinstrasse) sings its song for lovers of vintage clothing and fabulous homemade cakes and locally roasted java all in one convenient spot.

❸ Frosty Delights

Ice-cream parlour **Fräulein Frost** (📞030-9559 5521; Friedelstrasse 38; ⏱1pm-evening Mon-Fri, from noon Sat & Sun, closing time depends on weather; 📶; Ⓤ Schönleinstrasse) is all about experimentation, as reflected in such concoctions as apple-ginger or GuZiMi,which stands for Gurke-Zitrone-Minze (cucumber-lemon-mint).

❹ Burger Bonanza

The folks at **Berlin Burger International** (📞0160 482 6505; www.berlin-burgerinternational.com; Pannierstrasse 5; burgers €7-10.50; ⏱noon-11pm Mon-Thu, to midnight Fri & Sat, to 10pm Sun; 📶; Ⓤ Hermannplatz) know that size matters. At least when it comes to burgers: handmade, two-fisted, bulging and sloppy contenders.

❺ Weserstrasse Imbibing

This is the main drag to feed your party animal, with an eclectic mix of pubs and bars. Top picks include beers at **Ä** (📞030-3064 8751; www.ae-neukoelln.de; Weserstrasse 40; ⏱5pm-3am Mon-Sat, to midnight Sun; 🚌M41, Ⓤ Rathaus Neukölln), wine at **Vin Aqua Vin** (📞030-9405 2886; www.vinaquavin.de; Weserstrasse 204; ⏱4pm-midnight or later Mon-Wed, from 3pm Thu & Fri, from 2pm Sat; 🚌171, M29, M41, Ⓤ Hermannplatz) or cocktails at **Thelonius** (📞030-5561 8232; www.facebook.com/thelonious-barberlin; Weserstrasse 202; ⏱7pm-1am or later; Ⓤ Hermannplatz).

❻ Divine Baklava

Damaskus Konditorei (📞030-7037 0711; www.facebook.com/Konditorei. Damaskus; Sonnenallee 93; snacks from €2; ⏱9am-9pm Mon-Sat, 11.30am-8pm Sun; 🚌M41, Ⓤ Rathaus Neukölln) stands out for its artistic and rave-worthy pastries.Try the rich *kanafeh* (cheese-filled pastry drenched in syrup) or signature *halawat al jubn* (rosewater cheese pockets).

❼ Rooftop Chilling

During the warmer months, the club-garden-bar combo **Klunker-kranich** (www.klunkerkranich.de; Karl-Marx-Strasse 66; ⏱4pm-2am; 📶; Ⓤ Rathaus Neukölln) is a fab place for day-drinking and chilling to local DJs or bands. It's up on the rooftop parking deck of the Neukölln Arcaden shopping mall.

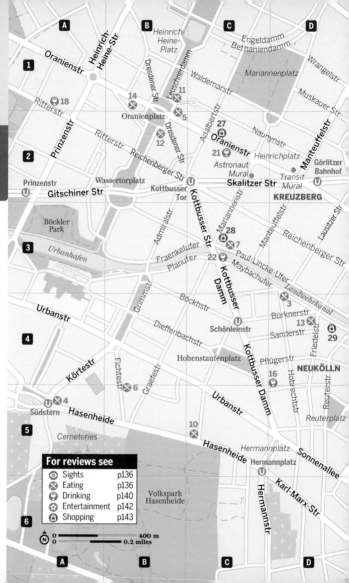

A **B** **C** **D**

Oranienstr

Heinrich-Heine-Str

Heinrich-Heine-Platz

Engeldamm

Bethaniendamm

Wrangelstr

1

Ritterstr

🚇18

Leuschnerdamm

Dresdener Str

Waldemarstr

Marianenplatz

Muskauer Str

14

Oranienplatz

5

11

Adalbertstr

27

Oranienstr

Naunynstr

Manteuffelstr

Ritterstr

Reichenberger Str

12

Dresdener Str

21

Heinrichplatz

Görlitzer Bahnhof

Prinzenstr

2

Prinzenstr

🚇

Gitschiner Str

Wassertorplatz

Kottbusser Tor

🚇

Astronaut Mural

Skalitzer Str

Transit Mural

KREUZBERG

Lausitzer Str

Böckler Park

3

Urbanhafen

Admiralstr

Fraenkelufer

Planufer

28

7

22

Marannenstr

Kottbusser Str

Paul-Lincke-Ufer

Maybachufer

Kottbusser Damm

Manteuffelstr

Reichenberger Str

Landwehrkanal

3

Urbanstr

Grimmstr

Böckhstr

Dieffenbachstr

Schönleinstr

🚇

Bürknerstr

13

Sanderstr

Friedelstr

29

Körtestr

Fichtestr

Graefestr

Hohenstaufenplatz

Pflügerstr

NEUKÖLLN

6

16

Hobrechtstr

Reuterstr

Reuterplatz

🚇4

Südstern

Hasenheide

Cemeteries

5

10

Hasenheide

Hermannplatz

Hermannplatz

🚇

Sonnenallee

Karl-Marx-Str

Hermannstr

For reviews see	
⊙ Sights	p136
⊗ Eating	p136
♀ Drinking	p140
★ Entertainment	p142
🔒 Shopping	p143

Volkspark Hasenheide

🇳 0 ——— 400 m
0 ——— 0.2 miles

6

A **B** **C** **D**

E
F
G
H

Mühlenstr
Spree River

Köpenicker Str

Warschauer Str
Warschauer Str
Warschauer Platz
Warschauer Str
Rudolfstr
Ehrenbergstr

1

Pücklerstr
Eisenbahnstr
Zeughofstr
Wrangelstr

2 26 15
Spreewaldplatz

Oberbaumstr
Oberbaumbrücke
Stralauer Allee

2

Schlesisches Tor
9
20
Pink Man Mural

Skalitzer Str
Yellow Man Mural
Rounded Heads Mural

Lübbener Str
Oppelner Str
23
25
Schlesische Str
Curvystr

Vor dem Schlesischen Tor
Am Flutgraben
Badeschiff
Osthafen

Uhlaustr Str
4
Wiener Str
Görlitzer Park
Görlitzer Str
Falckensteinstr
Taborstr
Heckmannufer
Görlitzer Ufer

19
Am Flutgraben
17
1
3

Reichenberger Str
Glogauer Str
Ratiborstr
Am Flutgraben
Schlesischer Busch
Puschkinallee
Eichenstr

Nansenstr
Ratiborstr
Lohmühlenstr
TREPTOW
Kiefholzstr
Am Treptower Park
Bouchéstr

4

Schmollerplatz
Karl-Kunger-Str
Kiefholzstr

Pannierstr
Heidelberger Str
Eisenstr

5

Weichselstr
Fuldastr
8
Elbestr
Harzer Str
Neuköllner Schifffahrtskanal

Sonnenallee
Weserstr
Wildenbruchstr
Weigandufer
Innstr
Kiehlufer

6

E
F
G
H

Sights

Badeschiff

SWIMMING

1 ⊙ MAP P134, H3

Take an old river barge, fill it with water, moor it in the Spree and – voila! – you get an artist-designed urban lifestyle pool that is a popular swim-and-chill spot. With music blaring, a sandy beach, wooden decks, lots of hot bods and a bar to fuel the fun, the vibe is distinctly 'Ibiza on the Spree'. Come early on scorching days as it's often filled to capacity (1500 people max) by noon. (☎0162 545 1374; www.arena-berlin.de; Eichenstrasse 4; adult/concession €5.50/3; ☉8am-varies (weather dependent) May-early Sep; 🚌265, 🚊Treptower Park, Ⓤschlesisches Tor)

Eating

Sironi

BAKERY €

2 ⊗ MAP P134, E2

The focaccia and ciabatta are as good as they get without taking a flight to Italy, thanks to Alfredo Sironi, who hails from the Boot and now treats Berlin bread lovers to his habit-forming carb creations. Watch the flour magicians whip up the next batch in his glass bakery right in the iconic Markthalle Neun (p143), then order a piece to go. (www.facebook.com/sironi.de; Eisenbahnstrasse 42, Markthalle Neun; snacks from €2.50; ☉8am-8pm Mon-Wed, Fri & Sat, to 10pm Thu; ⓊGörlitzer Bahnhof)

Cafe Jacques

MEDITERRANEAN €€

3 ⊗ MAP P134, D4

Like a fine wine, this darling French-Mediterranean lair keeps improving with age. Candlelit wooden tables and art-festooned brick walls feel as welcoming as an old friend's embrace. And indeed, a welcoming embrace from charismatic owner-host Ahmad may well await. The menu is a rotating festival of flavours, including mouthwatering meze, homemade pasta and fresh fish. (☎030-694 1048; http://cafejacques.de; Maybachufer 14; mains €12.50-19; ☉6pm-late; ⓊSchönleinstrasse)

Fes Turkish Barbecue

TURKISH €€

4 ⊗ MAP P134, A5

If you like a DIY approach to dining, give this innovative Turkish restaurant a try. Perhaps borrowing a page from the Koreans, it requires you to cook your own slabs of marinated chicken, beef fillet and tender lamb on a grill sunk right into your table. (☎030-2391 7778; http://fes-turkishbbq.de; Hasenheide 58; meze €4-10, meat from €15; ☉5-10pm Tue-Sun; ⓊSüdstern)

Orania

GERMAN €€€

5 ⊗ MAP P134, B2

Punctilious artisanship meets boundless creativity at Orania, where a small army of chefs fusses around culinary wunderkind Philipp Vogel in the shiny open kitchen. The flair is cosmo-chic with food and cocktails to match. Only three ingredients find their destiny in each product-focused dish, inspired by global flavours rather than the latest trends and often served with live music in the background. (☎030-6953 9680; https://orania.berlin/restaurant; Oranienstrasse 40; mains €30-36; ⏱6-11pm; Ⓤ Moritzplatz)

Tulus Lotrek
INTERNATIONAL €€€

6 ⊗ MAP P134, B5

Artist Henri de Toulouse-Lautrec was a bon vivant who embraced good food and wine, which is exactly what owner-chef Maximilian Strohe and owner-mâitre Ilona Scholl want their guests to do. With several awards and a Michelin star under their belts, the charismatic couple dishes up intellectually ambitious food with soul. (☎030-4195 6687; www.tuluslotrek.de; Fichtestrasse 24; 6-/7-/8-course

dinner €99/110/119; ⏱7pm-midnight Fri-Tue; 🥢; Ⓤ Südstern)

Horváth
AUSTRIAN €€€

7 ⊗ MAP P134, C3

At his canal-side restaurant, Sebastian Frank performs culinary alchemy with Austrian classics, fearlessly combining products, textures and flavours. The stunning results have earned him two Michelin stars and the title of Best Chef of Europe 2018. Wines are fabulous, of course, but Frank is also proud of his food-matching nonalcoholic beverage line-up, including tea infusions, vegetable juices and reductions. (☎030-6128 9992; www.restaurant-horvath.de; Paul-Lincke-Ufer 44a; 5-/7-/9-course menu €100/120/140; ⏱6-11pm Wed-Sun; Ⓤ Kottbusser Tor)

Kreuzberg & Neukölln Eating

Cafe Jacques (p136)

AGENCJA FOTOGRAFICZNA CARO/ALAMY STOCK PHOTO ©

eins44

FRENCH, GERMAN €€€

8 MAP P134, F6

This casual fine-dining outpost in a late-19th-century distillery serves meals with a strong native identity, composed largely with seasonally hunted and gathered ingredients. Metal lamps, tiles and heavy wooden tables beautifully match the industrial charm of the building. Lunches feature just a few classics, while dinners are multicourse dine-and-wine celebrations. (☑030-6298 1212; www.eins44.com; Elbestrasse 28/29, 2nd courtyard; mains lunch €8-10, dinner €26, 3-course dinner €49; ☺12.30-2.30pm Tue-Fri, 7pm-midnight Tue-Sat; ☎; ⌨M41, 104, 167, ⓤRathaus Neukölln)

Burgermeister

BURGERS €

9 MAP P134, F2

It's green, ornate, a century old and...it used to be a toilet. Now it's a super-popular burger joint beneath the elevated U-Bahn tracks. Get in line for the plump all-beef patties (try the Meisterburger with fried onions, bacon and barbecue sauce) tucked between a brioche bun and paired with thickly cut cheese fries. Fast-food heaven! (☑030-2388 3840; www.burger-meister.de; Oberbaumstrasse 8; burgers €3.50-4.80; ☺11am-3am Mon-Thu, 11am-4am Fri, noon-4am Sat, noon-3am Sun; ⓤSchlesisches Tor)

Top Five Kreuzberg Murals

Berlin has emerged as European street-art capital where some major local and international talent have left their mark on the city. Check out these five landmark murals.

Astronaut/Kosmonaut (Map p134, C2; Mariannenstrasse, near Skalitzer Strasse; ⓤKottbusser Tor) Victor Ash's monumental stencil-style piece was inspired by the US-Soviet space race.

Pink Man (Map p134, G2; Falckensteinstrasse 48; ⓤSchlesisches Tor) House-sized mural by Blu depicts a creature composed of hundreds of writhing pink bodies, plus a lone white guy crouched on its finger.

Rounded Heads (Map p134, F2; Oppelner Strasse 46-47; ⓤSchlesisches Tor) Internationally renowned Berlin street artist Nomad created this faceless person embracing a hooded character.

Yellow Man (Map p134, F2; Oppelner Strasse 3; ⓤSchlesisches Tor) This bizarrely dressed, seemingly genderless, yellow-skinned figure is a signature work by Brazilian twins Os Gemeos.

Transit (Map p134, D2; cnr Oranienstrasse & Manteuffelstrasse; ⓤGörlitzer Bahnhof) With his animal carcasses Belgian artist ROA illustrates the cycle of life and death in a distinctive monochrome spray-paint style.

Masaniello

ITALIAN €

10 ⊗ MAP P134, C5

The tables are almost too small for the wagon-wheel-sized certified Neapolitan pizzas tickled by wood fire at Luigi and Pascale's old-school but much-adored pizzeria. The crust is crispy, the tomato sauce has just the right amount of tang, and the toppings are piled on generously. (☏030-692 6657; www.masaniello.de; Hasenheide 20; pizza €6.50-11; ⊗noon-midnight; Ⓤ Hermannplatz)

Henne

GERMAN €

11 ⊗ MAP P134, B1

This Old Berlin institution operates on the KISS (keep it simple, stupid!) principle: milk-fed chicken spun on the rotisserie for moist yet crispy perfection. That's all it's been serving for over a century, alongside tangy potato and white cabbage salads. Eat in the garden or in the cosy 1907 dining room that's resisted the tides of time. Reservations essential. (☏030-614 7730; www.henne-berlin.de; Leuschnerdamm 25; half chicken €9.40; ⊗5pm-midnight Tue-Sun; ☒M29, 140, 147, Ⓤ Moritzplatz, Kottbusser Tor)

Ora

INTERNATIONAL €€

12 ⊗ MAP P134, B2

A 19th-century pharmacy has been splendidly rebooted as this stylishly casual cafe-bar-restaurant. The antique wooden medicine cabinets are now the back bar, where craft beer and cocktails are dispensed to a down-to-earth crowd with an appreciation for the finer things in life. The menu is modern brasserie food and makes deft use of seasonal and local ingredients. (http://ora-berlin.de; Oranienplatz 14; mains €8-15; ⊗noon-1am Mon-Fri, from 9.30am Sat & Sun; Ⓤ Kottbusser Tor)

Chicha

PERUVIAN €€

13 ⊗ MAP P134, D4

What began as a regular appearance at Berlin's street-food fairs has evolved into a cheerful permanent nosh spot serving such Peruvian classics as ceviche (marinated raw fish), *tiradito* (Nikkei-style tuna carpaccio) and *palmitos aparrillados* (grilled palm hearts). It all pairs perfectly with a tangy pisco sour and the cheerful decor. (☏030-6273 1010; www.chicha-berlin.de; Friedelstrasse 34; mains €8-13.50; ⊗6pm-midnight Wed-Sun; Ⓤ Schönleinstrasse)

Max und Moritz

GERMAN €€

14 ⊗ MAP P134, B1

The patina of yesteryear hangs over this ode-to-old-school gastropub, named for the cheeky Wilhelm Busch cartoon characters. Since 1902, it has packed hungry diners and thirsty drinkers into its rustic tile-and-stucco-ornamented rooms for sudsy home-brews and granny-style Berlin fare. A menu favourite is the *Königsberger Klopse* (veal meatballs in caper sauce). (☏030-6951 5911; www.maxundmoritzberlin.de; Oranienstrasse 162; mains €11.50-17; ⊗5pm-midnight; 🛜; Ⓤ Moritzplatz)

Drinking

Schwarze Traube COCKTAIL BAR

15 😊 MAP P134, E2

Mixologist Atalay Aktas was Germany's Best Bartender of 2013 and hasn't lost a step since. He and his staff still create their magic potions in this pint-sized drinking parlour with living-room looks. There's no menu, meaning each drink is calibrated to the taste and mood of each patron using premium spirits, expertise and a dash of psychology. (☏030-2313 5569; www. schwarzetraube.de; Wrangelstrasse 24; ⏱7pm-2am Sun-Thu, to 5am Fri & Sat; Ⓤ Görlitzer Bahnhof)

Geist im Glass BAR

16 😊 MAP P134, D4

Weekends wouldn't be the same without Aishah Bennett's soul-restoring brunches (killer pancakes, great Bloody Marys), but swinging by this seductively lit, cabin-style lair to get comfortable with immaculate cocktails and well-curated craft beer and wine selections is a clever endeavour any day. Quality is tops and prices fair. (☏0176 5533 0450; http://geist-im-glas.business.site; Lenaustrasse 27; ⏱7pm-2am Mon-Thu, 10am-4pm Fri, 7am-2am Fri & Sat, 10am-midnight Sun; Ⓤ Hermannplatz)

Club der Visionäre CLUB

17 😊 MAP P134, H3

It's cold beer, crispy pizza and fine electro at this summertime day-to-night-and-back-to-day chill and party playground in an old canal-side boat shed. Park yourself beneath the weeping willows, stake out some turf on the upstairs deck or hit the tiny dance floor. Alternatively, head to the sun deck of CDV's nearby second venue, the Hoppetoose boat, which doubles as a winter location. (☏030-6951 8942; www.clubdervisionaere.com; Am Flutgraben 1; ⏱2pm-late Mon-Fri, from noon Sat & Sun; Ⓢ Treptower Park, Ⓤ Schlesisches Tor)

Ritter Butzke CLUB

18 😊 MAP P134, A1

Ritter Butzke has origins as an illegal club but is now a Kreuzberg party circuit fixture. Wrinkle-free folk hit the four floors in a former bathroom-fittings factory for high-quality music, courtesy of both DJ legends and the latest sound spinners of the house and techno scenes. It also hosts concerts and there's a courtyard in summer. (www.ritterbutzke.de; Ritterstrasse 24; ⏱midnight-late Thu-Sat; Ⓤ Moritzplatz)

Birgit&Bier CLUB

19 😊 MAP P134, H3

Enter through the iron gate and embark on a magical mystery tour that'll have you chilling in the beer garden, taking selfies with wacky art, dancing under the disco ball and lounging in a retired carousel. An eclectic roster of events, including outdoor cinema, deep-flow music yoga and magical party nights, pretty much guarantees a good time. (📞030-618 7240; www.facebook.com/birgitundbier; Schleusenufer 3; 🕑2pm-5am Mon-Wed, to 6am Thu, to noon Fri & Sat, to 6am Sun; 🚌165, 265, N65, Ⓢ Treptower Park, ⓊSchlesisches Tor)

Watergate
CLUB

20 🚇 MAP P134, G2

For a short night's journey into day, check into this high-octane riverside club with two floors, panoramic windows and a floating terrace overlooking the Oberbaumbrücke and Universal Music. Top DJs keep electro-hungry hipsters hot and sweaty till way past sunrise. Long queues, tight door. (📞030-6128 0394; www.water-gate.de; Falckensteinstrasse 49a; 🕑midnight-5am or later Wed-Sat; ⓊSchlesisches Tor)

SO36
CLUB

21 🚇 MAP P134, C2

This legendary club began as an artist squat in the early 1970s and soon evolved into Berlin's seminal punk venue, known for wild concerts by the Dead Kennedys, Die Ärzte and Einstürzende Neubauten. Today the crowd depends on the night's program: electro party, punk concert, lesbigay tea dance, night flea market, '80s, 'Bad Taste' – pretty much anything goes. Easy door. (📞030-6140 1306; www.so36.de; Oranienstrasse 190; 🕑Mon-Sun; ⓊKottbusser Tor)

Ankerklause
PUB

22 🚇 MAP P134, C3

Ahoy there! Drop anchor at this nautical-kitsch tavern in an old

Club der Visionäre

KitKatClub

This 'kitty' is naughty, sexy and decadent, listens to electro of all stripes and fancies extravagant getups (or nothing at all). **KitKatClub** (www.kitkatclub.de; Köpenicker Strasse 76; ⏱11pm-late Fri, Sat & Mon, from 8am Sun; Ⓤ Heinrich-Heine-Strasse), Berlin's most (in)famous erotic nightclub hides out at Sage Club with its four dance floors, shimmering pool and fire-breathing dragon. The Saturday-night CarneBall Bizarre party is a classic among Berlin's hedonistic havens. The website has dress-code tips.

harbour master's shack and enjoy the arse-kicking jukebox, cold beers and surprisingly good German pub fare. The best seats are on the geranium-festooned terrace, where you can wave at the tourist boats puttering along the canal. A cult pit stop from breakfast until the wee hours. (📞030-693 5649; www.ankerk lause.de; Kottbusser Damm 104; ⏱4pm-late Mon, from 10am Tue-Sun; Ⓤ Schönleinstrasse)

Hopfenreich
PUB

23 ⭐ MAP P134, F2

Since 2014, Berlin's first dedicated craft-beer bar has been plying punters with a changing roster of 22 global ales, IPAs and other brews on tap – both known and obscure. It's all served with street-cred flourish in a corner pub near the Schlesische Strasse party mile. (📞030-8806 1080; www.hopfenreich. de; Sorauer Strasse 31; ⏱4pm-2am Mon-Thu, to 3am Fri-Sun; Ⓤ Schlesisches Tor)

Entertainment

Wild at Heart
LIVE MUSIC

24 ⭐ MAP P134, E3

Named after a David Lynch road movie, this kitsch-cool dive with blood-red walls, tiki gods and Elvis paraphernalia hammers home punk, ska, surf-rock and rockabilly. It's really, REALLY loud, so if your ears need a break, head to the tiki-themed restaurant-bar next door. Free concerts on Wednesday. (📞030-611 9231; www. wildatheartberlin.de; Wiener Strasse 20; ⏱8pm-late Wed-Sun; Ⓤ Görlitzer Bahnhof)

Lido
LIVE MUSIC

25 ⭐ MAP P134, G2

A 1950s cinema has been recycled into a rock-indie-electro-pop hub with mosh-pit electricity and a crowd that cares more about the music than about looking good. Global DJs and talented upwardly mobile live noisemakers pull in the punters. Its monthly Balkanbeats party is legendary. (📞030-6956 6840; www.lido-berlin.de; Cuvrystrasse 7; Ⓤ Schlesisches Tor)

Shopping

Markthalle Neun
MARKET

26 🔒 MAP P134, E2

This delightful 1891 market hall with its iron-beam-supported ceiling was saved by dedicated locals in 2009. On market days, local and regional producers present their wares, while on **Street Food Thursday** (www.markthalleneun.de; Eisenbahnstrasse 42-43; 🕘5-10pm Thu; Ⓤ Görlitzer Bahnhof), a couple of dozen international amateur or semipro chefs set up their stalls to serve delicious snacks from around the world. There's even an on-site craft brewery, Heidenpeters. (☏030-6107 3473; www.markthalleneun.de; Eisenbahnstrasse 42-43; 🕘noon-6pm Mon-Wed & Fri, noon-10pm Thu, 10am-6pm Sat; Ⓤ Görlitzer Bahnhof)

VooStore
FASHION & ACCESSORIES

27 🔒 MAP P134, C2

Kreuzberg's first concept store opened in an old backyard locksmith shop off gritty Oranienstrasse, stocking style-forward designer threads and accessories by a changing roster of crave-worthy brands, along with a tightly curated spread of books, gadgets, mags and spirits. The in-house Companion Cafe serves specialty coffees and tea from micro farms. (☏030-6165 1112; www.vooberlin.com; Oranienstrasse 24; 🕘10am-8pm Mon-Sat; Ⓤ Kottbusser Tor)

Hard Wax
MUSIC

28 🔒 MAP P134, C3

This well-hidden outpost has been on the cutting edge of electronic music for about two decades and is a must-stop for fans of techno, house, minimal, dubstep and whatever permutation comes along next. (☏030-6113 0111; www.hardwax.com; Paul-Lincke-Ufer 44a, 3rd fl, door A, 2nd courtyard; 🕘noon-8pm Mon-Sat; Ⓤ Kottbusser Tor)

Nowkoelln Flowmarkt
MARKET

29 🔒 MAP P134, D4

This flea market sets up twice-monthly along the scenic Landwehrkanal and delivers secondhand bargains galore along with handmade threads and jewellery. (www.nowkoelln.de; Maybachufer; 🕘10am-6pm 2nd & 4th Sun of month Mar-Oct or later; Ⓤ Kottbusser Tor, Schönleinstrasse)

Explore
Friedrichshain

The former East Berlin district of Friedrichshain is famous for such high-profile Cold War–era relics as the longest surviving stretch of Berlin Wall (the East Side Gallery), the socialist boulevard Karl-Marx-Allee and the former Stasi headquarters. But the area also stakes it reputation on having Berlin's most rambunctious nightlife scene, with a glut of clubs and bars holding forth along Revaler Strasse and around the Ostkreuz train station.

Confront the ghosts of the Cold War on a stroll along the East Side Gallery (p146), then pop into Michelberger (p151) for a late breakfast or early lunch. Energies renewed, sample the monumentalism of Karl-Marx-Allee (p150) on a short stroll before delving deep into the East German underbelly at the Stasimuseum (p152). Finish the afternoon poking into boho boutiques around Boxhagener Platz (p150), then head to the RAW Gelände (p156) to chill in the beer garden at Cassiopeia (p156) or Urban Spree (p150). Gear up for a night of dance-floor shenanigans at Berghain (p154), if you're lucky to get in, with dinner at trendy riverside Katerschmaus (p153).

Getting There & Around

S Ostbahnhof and Warschauer Strasse are handy for the East Side Gallery; Warschauer Strasse and Ostkreuz for Boxhagener Platz and Revaler Strasse.

U U1 links Warschauer Strasse with Kreuzberg, Schöneberg and Charlottenburg; the U5 runs from Alexanderplatz down Karl-Marx-Allee and beyond.

🚊 M10 and M13 link Warschauer Strasse with Prenzlauer Berg

Friedrichshain Map on p148

Flohmarkt am Boxhagener Platz (p157) TRAVELPIX/ALAMY STOCK PHOTO ©

Top Sight 📷
East Side Gallery

The year was 1989. After 28 years the Berlin Wall, that grim divider of humanity, met its maker. Most of it was quickly dismantled, but a 1.3km stretch along Mühlenstrasse, between Oberbaumbrücke and Ostbahnhof, became the East Side Gallery, the world's largest open-air mural strip. Today it's a memorial to the fall of the Wall and the peaceful reunification that followed.

◎ MAP P148, B5

www.eastsidegallery-berlin.de

Mühlenstrasse btwn Oberbaumbrücke & Ostbahnhof

admission free

🕑 24hr

Ⓤ Warschauer Strasse,
Ⓢ Ostbahnhof, Warschauer Strasse

Dmitri Vrubel: My God, Help Me To Survive This Deadly Love

The gallery's best-known painting – showing Soviet and GDR leaders Leonid Brezhnev and Erich Honecker locking lips with eyes closed – is based on an actual photograph taken by French journalist Remy Bossu during Brezhnev's 1979 Berlin visit. This kind of fraternal kiss was an expression of great respect in socialist countries.

Birgit Kinder: Test the Rest

Another shutterbug favourite is Kinder's painting of a GDR-era Trabant car (known as a Trabi) bursting through the Wall with the licence plate reading 'November 9, 1989'. Originally called Test the Best, the artist renamed her work after the image's 2009 restoration.

Kani Alavi: It Happened in November

A wave of people being squeezed through a breached Wall in a metaphorical rebirth reflects Alavi's recollection of the events of 9 November 1989. Note the different expressions on the faces, ranging from hope, joy and euphoria to disbelief and fear.

Thierry Noir: Homage to the Young

This Berlin-based French artist has done work for Wim Wenders and U2, but he's most famous for these cartoon-like heads. Naive, simple and boldly coloured, they symbolise the new-found freedom that followed the Wall's collapse. Noir was one of the few artists who had painted the western side of the Wall before its demise.

Thomas Klingenstein: Detour to the Japanese Sector

Born in East Berlin, Klingenstein spent time in a Stasi prison for dissent before being extradited to West Germany in 1980. This mural was inspired by his childhood love for Japan, where he ended up living from 1984 to the mid-'90s.

★ Top Tips

○ The more famous paintings are near the Ostbahnhof end, so start here if you've got limited time.

○ For more street art and graffiti, check out the river-facing side of the East Side Gallery.

○ The grassy strip between the gallery and Spree River is a nice spot for chilling with a picnic or a cold beer. There are supermarkets in the Ostbahnhof.

✗ Take a Break

○ The Floating Lounge bar at the **Eastern Comfort Hostelboat** (Mühlenstrasse 73; U Warschauer Strasse, S Warschauer Strasse) is a great spot for a drink. Sit on the sun deck in summer.

○ On weekdays, mingle with Universal Music staff on the lovely riverside terrace of the **Eatside** (☏ 030-520 071 823; www.eat-side.de; Stralauer Allee 1; mains €6.50-7.50; ☷ 11.30am-3pm Mon-Fri; ☎ ✐; S Warschauer Strasse, U Warschauer Strasse) bistro.

Friedrichshain

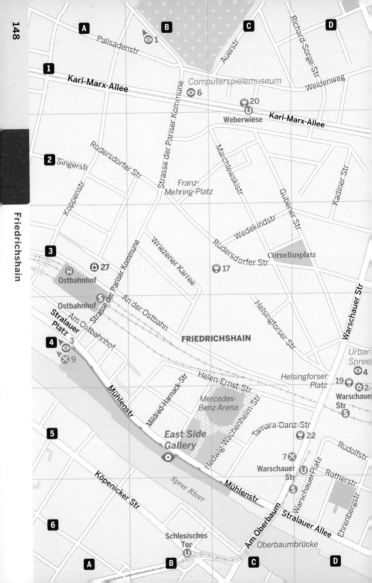

A
B
C
D

Palisadenstr

1 ⊙ 1

1 Karl-Marx-Allee

Computerspielemuseum

⊙ 6

⊙ 20
Ⓤ

Weberwiese
Karl-Marx-Allee

Auerstr

Richard-Sorge-Str

Weidenweg

Rüdersdorfer Str

2 Singerstr

Koppenstr

Strasse der Pariser Kommune

Franz-
Mehring-Platz

Marchlewskistr

Wedekindstr

Gubener Str

Kadiner Str

3

🏛 ⛫ 27
Ostbahnhof

Ⓢ

Wriezener Karree

Rüdersdorfer Str

Corneliusplatz

⊙ 17

Helsingforser Str

Warschauer Str

Ostbahnhof
Ⓢ
Stralauer
Platz

An der Ostbahn

Strasse der Pariser Kommune

Am Ostbahnhof

FRIEDRICHSHAIN

4 ⊙ 3
✕ 9

Mühlenstr

Mildred-Harnack-Str

Helen-Ernst-Str

Mercedes-
Benz Arena

Hedwig-Wachenheim-Str

Helsingforser
Platz

19 ⊙ ⊙ 2
Warschauer
Str
Ⓢ

Urban
Spree
⊙ 4

5

East Side
Gallery
⊙

Tamara-Danz-Str

⊙ 22

7 ✕
Warschauer
Str
Ⓤ

Warschauer Platz

Rudolfstr

Rotherstr

Ehrenbergstr

Köpenicker Str

Spree River

Mühlenstr

Ⓢ

6

Schlesisches
Tor
Ⓤ

Am Oberbaum

Stralauer Allee

Oberbaumbrücke

A
B
C
D

E F G H

Petersburger Str

Banschstr

Rigaer Str

Proskauer Str

N
0   400 m
0   0.2 miles

1

Karl-Marx-Allee

Frankfurter Tor
Ⓤ

2 ◎

Frankfurter Allee

Ⓤ Samariterstr

2

Warschauer Str

Niederbarnimstr

Mainzer Str

Scharnweberstr

Weichselstr

Boxhagener Str

Grünberger Str

Simon-Dach-Str

13 ✖

Gabriel-Max-Str

Boxhagener Platz

26 🔒 ◎ 5

Gärtnerstr

Krossener Str

Traveplatz

14 ✖

3

Weserstr

Jessnerstr

Kopernikusstr

✖ 8

Wühlischstr

23 🍷 16 ✖

Simon-Dach-Str

Gärtnerstr

Seumestr

Weserstr

4

12 ✖

Simplonstr

25 🔒   10 ✖

21 🍷

Revaler Str

Sonntagstr

Lenbachstr

11 ✖

Neue Bahnhofstr

Markstrasse

5

Weichselstr

15 ✖

Simplonstr

Rudolfplatz

Modersohnstr

Markgrafendamm

18 🍷

Ostkreuz
Ⓢ

6

Corinthstr

E F G H

Friedrichshain

Sights

Volkspark Friedrichshain
PARK

1 MAP P148, B1

Berlin's oldest public park has provided relief from urbanity since 1840, but has been hilly only since the late 1940s, when wartime debris was piled up here to create two 'mountains' – the taller one, **Mont Klamott**, rises 78m high. Diversions include expansive lawns for lazing, tennis courts, a half-pipe for skaters, a couple of handily placed beer gardens and an outdoor cinema. (bounded by Am Friedrichshain, Friedenstrasse, Danziger Strasse & Landsberger Allee; ⏰24hr; 🚌142, 200, 🚊21, M4, M5, M6, M8, M10, USchillingstrasse)

Karl-Marx-Allee
STREET

2 MAP P148, E2

It's easy to feel like Gulliver in the Land of Brobdingnag when walking down monumental Karl-Marx-Allee, one of Berlin's most impressive GDR-era relics. Built between 1952 and 1960, the 90m-wide boulevard runs for 2.3km between Alexanderplatz and Frankfurter Tor and is a fabulous showcase of East German architecture. A considerable source of national pride back then, it provided modern flats for comrades and served as a backdrop for military parades. (admission free; UStrausberger Platz, Weberwiese, Frankfurter Tor)

Holzmarkt
AREA

3 MAP P148, A4

The Holzmarkt urban village on the Spree is a perpetually evolving cultural open playground – and a nose-thumbing at the luxury lofts, hotels and office buildings that continue to gobble up the riverside real estate. (www.holzmarkt.com; Holzmarktstrasse 25; UJannowitzbrücke)

Urban Spree
ARTS CENTRE

4 MAP P148, D4

Comprising a gallery, a bookshop, artist studios, a concert room and a beer garden, this grassroots urban art hub is a top stop in the RAW Gelände (p156) compound along Revaler Strasse, especially in summer. That's also when it hosts festivals and special events and presents Berlin's best street musicians on weekends. (📞030-740 7597; www.urbanspree.com; Revaler Strasse 99; ⏰noon-11pm; UWarschauer Strasse, SWarschauer Strasse)

Boxhagener Platz
SQUARE

5 MAP P148, F3

The heart of Friedrichshain, 'Boxi' is a lovely, leafy square with benches and a playground. It's framed by restored 19th-century buildings harbouring boho cafes, artisanal bakeries and shabby-chic boutiques. The area is busiest during the Saturday **farmers' market** and on Sundays, when a flea market (p157) brings in folks from all over town. (Boxhagener Platz;

admission free; ⊙24hr; P; ☐240, S Warschauer Strasse, U Samariter-strasse, Warschauer Strasse)

Computerspiele-museum

MUSEUM

6 ◎ MAP P148, B1

No matter if you grew up with Nimrod, Pac-Man, World of Warcraft or no games at all, this well-curated museum takes you on a trip down computer-game memory lane while putting the industry's evolution into historical context. Colourful and engaging, it features interactive stations amid hundreds of exhibits, including an ultra-rare 1972 Pong arcade machine and its twisted modern cousin, the 'PainStation' (must be over 18 to play...). (Computer Games Museum; ☎030-6098

8577; www.computerspielemuseum, Karl-Marx-Allee 93a; adult/concession €9/6, after 6pm €7/5; ⊙10am-8pm; ☐240, 347, U Weberwiese)

Eating

Michelberger

INTERNATIONAL €€

7 ✖ MAP P148, C5

Ensconced in one of Berlin's hip-pest **hotels**, Michelberger makes creative dishes that often combine unusual organic ingredients (eg wild boar with miso, scallops, cabbage and gooseberry). Sit inside the lofty, white-tiled restaurant or in the breezy courtyard. (☎030-2977 8590; www.michelbergerhotel.com; Warschau-er Strasse 39; 3-course lunch €12, dinner dishes €8-15; ⊙7-11am, noon-2.30pm & 6.30-11pm; ☎☒; S Warschauer Strasse, U Warschauer Strasse)

Karl-Marx-Allee

ELXENEIZE/SHUTTERSTOCK ©

n 1950 and modelled after the Soviet KGB, East Germany's
m *für Staatssicherheit* (Ministry of State Security, 'Stasi'
for short) was secret police, central intelligence agency and bureau
of criminal investigation all rolled into one. It put millions of its own
citizens under surveillance in order to suppress internal opposition
and, by 1989, had 91,000 official full-time employees and 189,000
IMs (*inoffizielle Mitarbeiter*, unofficial informants). The latter were
regular folks recruited to spy on their coworkers, friends, family and
neighbours.

Stasi Museum

The often cunningly low-tech surveillance devices (hidden in
watering cans, rocks, even neckties) are among the more intriguing
exhibits in the **Stasimuseum** (☏030-553 6854; www.stasimuseum.de;
Haus 1, Ruschestrasse 103; adult/concession €6/4.50; ☉10am-6pm Mon-
Fri, 11am-6pm Sat & Sun, English tour 3pm Sat-Mon; Ⓤ Magdalenenstrasse)
inside the actual former Stasi ministry in Lichtenberg, just east
of Friedrichshain. Another highlight are the stuffy original offices,
private quarters and conference rooms of Erich Mielke, head of the
Stasi from 1957 until the end. Other rooms introduce the ideology,
rituals and institutions of East German society. Information panels
are partly in English. In the foyer is a van honeycombed with teensy,
lightless cells that was used to transport suspects to the nearby
Stasi prison.

Stasi Prison

Officially called **Gedenkstätte Berlin-Hohenschönhausen** (☏030-
9860 8230; www.stiftung-hsh.de; Genslerstrasse 66; tours adult/concession
€6/3, exhibit free; ☉tours in English 10.30am, 12.30pm & 2.30pm Mar-Oct,
11.30am & 2.30pm Nov-Feb, exhibit 9am-6pm, German tours more frequent;
Ⓟ; ⓜM5), the Stasi prison is, if anything, even more creepy than
the Stasi Museum. Tours, sometimes led by former prisoners, reveal
the full extent of the terror and cruelty perpetrated upon thousands
of suspected political opponents, many utterly innocent. If you've
seen the Academy Award–winning film *The Lives of Others*, you may
recognise many of the original settings. An exhibit uses photographs, objects and a free audio-guide to document daily life behind
bars and also allows for a look at the offices of the former prison
administration.

Silo Coffee

CAFE €

8 ⊗ MAP P148, F4

If you've greeted the day with bloodshot eyes, get back in gear at this Aussie-run coffee and breakfast joint favoured by Friedrichshain's hip and expat. Beans from Fjord coffee roasters ensure possibly the best flat white in town, while bread from Sironi (Markthalle Neun) adds scrumptiousness to the poached-egg avo toast. (www.facebook.com/silocoffee; Gabriel-Max-Strasse 4; dishes €6-12; ☺8.30am-5pm Mon-Fri, 9.30am-6pm Sat & Sun; 🛜🖋; 🚋M10, M13, Ⓤ Warschauer Strasse, Ⓢ Warschauer Strasse)

Katerschmaus

INTERNATIONAL €€€

9 ⊗ MAP P148, A4

From the homemade bread to the wicked crème brûlée, dining at this carefully designed ramshackle space under the U-Bahn tracks is very much a Berlin experience. The kitchen embraces the regional-seasonal credo and presents meaty, fishy or vegetarian multicourse dinners as well as à la carte dining. Reservations essential. (☎0152 2941 3262; www.katerschmaus.de; Holzmarktstrasse 25; multicourse dinners €50-80; ☺noon-4pm & 7-10.30pm Tue-Sat; 🛜; Ⓤ Jannowitzbrücke, Ⓢ Jannowitzbrücke)

Khwan

THAI, BARBECUE €€

10 ⊗ MAP P148, E4

For some of the best Thai barbecue this side of Bangkok, pounce upon this rustic lair ensconced – for now – among the clubs and bars on the RAW Gelände strip. Let your nose be hooked by the aromatic smoke (khwan in Thai) wafting from the wood grill, where flames lick chicken, pork, fish, lamb and vegetables to succulent smokiness. (☎0152 5902 1331; http://khwanberlin.com; Revaler Strasse 99; dishes €4.50-19; ☺6pm-late Tue-Sat; 🛜; 🚋M10, M13, Ⓤ Warschauer Strasse, Ⓢ Warschauer Strasse)

Vöner

VEGAN €

11 ⊗ MAP P148, H5

Vöner stands for 'vegan doner kebab' and is a spit-roasted blend of wheat protein, vegetables and herbs. It was dreamed up more than a 20 years ago by Holger Frerichs, a one-time resident of a so-called Wagenburg, a countercultural commune made up of old vans, buses and caravans. The alt-spirit lives on in his original Vöner outlet. (☎0176 9651 3869; www.facebook.com/Voener; Boxhagener Strasse 56; dishes €3.50-6.50; ☺noon-11pm; 🖋; Ⓢ Ostkreuz)

Schneeweiss

EUROPEAN €€

12 ⊗ MAP P148, F4

The chilly-chic snowy white decor, with an eye-catching 'ice' chandelier, complements the Alpine menu at this fine-dining pioneer in Friedrichshain. Although the emphasis is on such classics as schnitzel, goulash and spaetzle (mac' 'n' cheese), the chef's talents also shine through with seasonal specials. Reservations essential for weekend brunch. (📞030-2904 9704; www.schneeweiss-berlin.de; Simplonstrasse 16; mains €13-25, Sun brunch €15; ⏱10am-3pm & 6pm-1am Mon-Fri, 10am-1am Sat & Sun; 👶; 🚊M13, Ⓤ Warschauer Strasse, Ⓢ Warschauer Strasse)

Lemon Leaf   ASIAN €€

13 🍴 MAP P148, F3

Cheap, cheerful and stylish, this place is always swarmed by loyal locals, and for good reason: light, inventive and fresh, the South Asian menu goes beyond the standard dishes and has few false notes. Intriguing choice: the sweetsour Indochine salad with banana blossoms. (📞030-2900 9428; www.lemonleaf.de; Grünberger Strasse 69; mains €8-14; ⏱noon-midnight; 🛜🎫; 🚊M10, Ⓤ Frankfurter Tor)

Aunt Benny   AMERICAN €

14 🍴 MAP P148, H4

This daytime cafe in an unhurried yet central section of Friedrichshain combines urban sophistication with down-homey North American treats. Tuck into avo toast, a BLT sandwich or homemade carrot cake while catching up on chit chat or your reading (lots of international magazines). (📞030-6640 5300; www.facebook.com/auntbennyberlin; Oderstrasse 7, enter on Jessnerstrasse; mains €5-10; ⏱8.30am-6pm Tue-Fri, from 9am Sat & Sun; Ⓢ Frankfurter Allee, Ⓤ Frankfurter Allee)

Milja & Schäfa   CAFE €€

15 🍴 MAP P148, H5

Natural woods and an airy layout lend a Scandinavian vibe to this mellow cafe, where mouthwatering breakfast options are listed on a black-slate board behind the counter with cases full of homemade cakes. Much creativity goes into the pasta dishes and sharing plates as well. Bonus: sunny pavement seating. (📞030-5266 2094; www.facebook.com/MiljaundSchaefa; Sonntagstrasse 1; mains €11-21; ⏱8am-midnight Mon-Thu, 8am-1am Fri, 9am-1am Sat, 9am-6pm Sun; 🛜; Ⓢ Ostkreuz)

Spätzle & Knödel   GERMAN €€

16 🍴 MAP P148, F4

This elbows-on-the-table gastropub provides a southern German comfort-food fix, including roast pork with dark-beer gravy, goulash with red cabbage and, of course, the eponymous *spaetzle* (German mac' 'n' cheese) and Knödel (dumplings). Bonus: Bavarian Riegele, Maisel and Weihenstephan beers on tap. (📞030-2757 1151; www.spaetzleknoedel.de; Wühlischstrasse 20; mains €9-16; ⏱5-11pm; Ⓤ Samariterstrasse)

Drinking

Berghain/ Panorama Bar   CLUB

17 🍺 MAP P148, C3

Only world-class spin-masters heat up this hedonistic bass-junkie hellhole inside a labyrinthine ex-power plant. Hard-edged minimal techno dominates the ex-turbine hall (Berghain) while house dominates at Panorama Bar, one floor up. Long lines, strict door, no cameras. Check the website for midweek concerts and record-release parties at the main venue and the adjacent **Kantine am Berghain** (www.berghain.de; Am Wriezener Bahnhof; admission varies; ⏱hours vary; Ⓢ Ostbahnhof). (www.berghain.de; Am Wriezener Bahnhof; ⏱Fri-Mon; Ⓢ Ostbahnhof)

://about blank   CLUB

18 MAP P148, G6

At this gritty multifloor party pen with lots of nooks and crannies, a steady line-up of top DJs feeds a diverse bunch of revellers dance-worthy electronic gruel. Intense club nights usually segue into the morning and beyond. Run by a collective, the venue also hosts cultural, political and gender events. (www.aboutparty.net; Markgrafendamm 24c; ⏱hours vary, always Fri & Sat; Ⓢ Ostkreuz)

Suicide Circus   CLUB

19 MAP P148, D4

Resident and visitors hungry for an eclectic techno shower invade this midsize dancing den with its industrial warehouse feel, top-notch sound system and consistently capable DJs. In summer, watch the stars fade from the open-air floor and garden. It's still a great spot to connect with the earthy Berlin club flair. (http://suicide-berlin.com; Revaler Strasse 99; ⏱hours vary, often

Cassiopeia (p156)

EDEN BREITZ/ALAMY STOCK PHOTO ©

Urban Playground

The jumble of derelict buildings called **RAW Gelände** (along Revaler Strasse; $\boxed{S}$ Warschauer Strasse, Ostkreuz, $\boxed{U}$ Warschauer Strasse) is one of the last subcultural hubs in central Berlin. Founded in 1867 as a train repair station ('*Reichsbahn-Ausbesserungs-Werk*', aka RAW), it remained in operation until 1994. Since 1999 the graffiti-slathered grounds have been a thriving offbeat sociocultural centre for creatives of all stripes. They also harbour clubs, bars, a beer garden, an indoor skate park, a beach club, a bunker-turned-climbing-wall and a Sunday flea market.

from midnight Tue-Sun; $\boxed{S}$ Warschauer Strasse, $\boxed{U}$ Warschauer Strasse)

Briefmarken Weine WINE BAR

20 MAP P148, C1

For *dolce vita* right on socialist-era Karl-Marx-Allee, head to this charmingly nostalgic Italian wine bar ensconced in a former stamp shop. The original wooden cabinets cradle a hand-picked selection of Italian bottles that complement a snack menu of yummy cheeses, prosciutto and salami, plus a pasta dish of the day. Best to book ahead. (📞030-4202 5292; www.briefmarken weine.de; Karl-Marx-Allee 99; ⏱7pm-midnight Mon-Sat; $\boxed{U}$ Weberwiese)

Cassiopeia CLUB

21 MAP P148, E4

The down-to-earth crowd at this charmingly trashy dancing den defines the word eclectic, and so does the music. Dive deep into a sound spectrum ranging from vintage hip-hop to hard funk, '80s pop and punk to electronic beats, delivered both live and via DJs. It's in an industrial hall on the RAW Gelände, a train repair station turned subcultural party village. (www.cassiopeia-berlin.de; Revaler Strasse 99, Gate 2; ⏱from 7pm or later Tue-Sun; 🚊M10, M13, $\boxed{U}$ Warschauer Strasse, $\boxed{S}$ Warschauer Strasse)

Monster Ronson's Ichiban Karaoke KARAOKE

22 MAP P148, D5

Knock back a couple of brewskis if you need to loosen your nerves before belting out your best Adele or Lady Gaga at this mad, great karaoke joint, which went through a major rejuvenation in early 2018. Shy types can book a private booth for music and mischief. It also has gay-themed nights and drag queen shows on Tuesdays. (📞030-8975 1327; www.karaoke monster.de; Warschauer Strasse 34; ⏱7pm-4am; $\boxed{S}$ Warschauer Strasse, $\boxed{U}$ Warschauer Strasse)

Hops & Barley MICROBREWERY

23 MAP P148, F4

Conversation flows as freely as the unfiltered pilsner, malty *Dunkel* (dark) and fruity *Weizen* (wheat) produced right here at one of Berlin's oldest craft breweries (since 2008). The pub is inside a former butcher's shop and still has the tiled walls to prove it. Two beamers project football (soccer) games. (☎030-2936 7534; www.hopsandbarley-berlin.de; Wühlischstrasse 22/23; ☼5pm-late Mon-Fri, from 3pm Sat & Sun; 🚃M13, Ⓤ Warschauer Strasse, Ⓢ Warschauer Strasse)

Entertainment

Astra Kulturhaus
LIVE MUSIC

24 ⭐ MAP P148, D5

With space for 1500 in the former cultural hall of a Cold War–era train repair station, Astra is one of Berlin's bigger indie concert venues, yet it often fills up easily, and not just when international headliners hit the stage. In addition, parties lure punters with danceable tunes across the sound spectrum. (☎030-2005 6767; www.astra-berlin.de; Revaler Strasse 99, RAW Gelände; ☼hours vary, always Thu-Sat; 🚃M13, Ⓢ Warschauer Strasse, Ⓤ Warschauer Strasse)

Shopping

RAW Flohmarkt
MARKET

25 🔒 MAP P148, E4

Bargains abound at this smallish flea market right on the grounds of RAW Gelände (p156), a former train repair station-turned-party village. It's wonderfully free of professional sellers, meaning you'll find everything from the proverbial kitchen sink to 1970s go-go b... Bargains are plentiful, while s... food and a beer garden provid... handy post-shopping pit stops (www.raw-flohmarkt-berlin.de; Revaler Strasse 99, RAW Gelände; ☼9am-5pm Sun; 🚃M10, M13, Ⓢ Warschauer Strasse, Ⓤ Warschauer Strasse)

Flohmarkt am Boxhagener Platz
MARKET

26 🔒 MAP P148, F3

Wrapped around leafy Boxhagener Platz, this fun flea market is just a java whiff away from oodles of convivial cafes. Although the presence of pro vendors has grown, there's still plenty of regular folks here to unload their spring-cleaning detritus at bargain prices. (Boxhagener Platz; ☼10am-6pm Sun; 🚃M13, Ⓢ Warschauer Strasse, Ⓤ Warschauer Strasse, Samariterstrasse)

Antikmarkt am Ostbahnhof
ANTIQUES

Sunday only

27 🔒 MAP P148, A3

If you're after antiques and collectibles, head to this sprawling market outside the Ostbahnhof station's north exit. The Grosser Antikmarkt (large antiques market) is more professional and brims with old coins, Iron Curtain–era relics, gramophone records, books, stamps, jewellery, etc. It segues neatly into the Kleiner Antikmarkt (small antiques market), which has more bric-a-brac and lower prices. (Erich-Steinfurth-Strasse; ☼9am-5pm Sun; Ⓢ Ostbahnhof)

Explore ◉
Prenzlauer Berg

Splendidly well-groomed Prenzlauer Berg is one of Berlin's most charismatic residential neighbourhoods, filled with cafes, historic buildings and indie boutiques. On Sundays, the world descends on its Mauerpark for flea marketeering, karaoke and chilling. A visit here is easily combined with the Gedenkstätte Berliner Mauer (p96), a 1.4km-long exhibit that illustrates how the Berlin Wall shaped the city.

Kick off with a late breakfast at Anna Blume (p168) following by browsing eclectic indie boutiques around Kollwitzplatz. Learn about life in East Berlin at the Museum in der Kulturbrauerei (p164), then fortify yourself with a cult Currywurst (curried sausage) at Konnopke's Imbiss (p167) before steering towards the Mauerpark. Try to visualize what the park looked like when the Berlin Wall ran right through it, then ring in the evening below the towering chestnuts of Prater (p166), Berlin's oldest beer garden. For dinner, consider Umami (p165) for Vietnamese or German rib stickers at Zum Schusterjungen (p167), followed by out-there cocktails at Bryk Bar (p167).

Getting There & Around

Ⓤ The U2 stops at Schönhauser Allee, Eberswalder Strasse and Senefelderplatz.

🚊 The M1 links Museumsinsel and Prenzlauer Berg via the Scheunenviertel, Kastanienallee and Schönhauser Allee. The M13 heads to Friedrichshain.

Ⓢ Ringbahn (Circle Line) trains S41 and S42 stop at Schönhauser Allee, Greifswalder Strasse, Landberger Strasse and Storkower Strasse.

Prenzlauer Berg Map on p162

Mauerpark (p160) DI GREGORIO GIULIO/SHUTTERSTOCK ©

Walking Tour 🥾

Sundays Around the Mauerpark

Locals, expats and tourists – everyone flocks to the Mauerpark on Sundays. It's an energetic urban tapestry where a flea market, karaoke and bands provide entertainment, and people gather for barbecues, basketball and boules. A graffiti-covered section of the Berlin Wall recalls the time when the park was part of the death strip separating East and West Berlin.

Walk Facts

Start Oderberger Strasse, U-Bahn Eberswalder Strasse

End Northern Mauerpark, U-Bahn Schönhauser Allee

Length 1.7km, one hour without stops

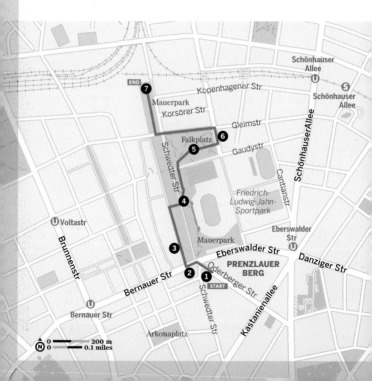

❶ Bright Beginnings

Start on Oderberger Strasse, which is lined with restaurants and cafes, including **Bonanza Coffee Heroes** (www.bonanzacoffee.de; Oderberger Strasse 35; ⏰8.30am-6pm Mon-Fri, 10am-6.30pm Sat & Sun; 🛜; 🚋M1, M10, 12, Ⓤ Eberswalder Strasse). Look up at the beautiful facades of the restored 19th-century townhouses that were saved from demolition in the late '70s when the street dead-ended at the Berlin Wall.

❷ Confronting Cold War History

During the Cold War, East met West at Bernauer Strasse, now paralleled by a 1.4km-long linear multimedia **memorial exhibit** (p96) that vividly illustrates the realities of life with the Berlin Wall. Its eastern terminus is here at Schwedter Strasse. Even walking just a short stretch west offers eye-opening insights.

❸ Urban Archaeology

Hit the **Flohmarkt im Mauerpark** (www.flohmarktimmauerpark.de; Bernauer Strasse 63-64; ⏰9am-6pm Sun; 🚋M1, M10, 12, Ⓤ Eberswalder Strasse) for some quality hunting and gathering of retro threads, cool stuff by local designers and vintage vinyl. Afterwards, fortify yourself at a street-food stall or listen to the buskers in the park.

❹ Bearpit Karaoke

On most summer Sundays, Berlin's best free entertainment kicks off around 3pm when Joe Hatchiban sets up his custom-made mobile karaoke unit in the Mauerpark's amphitheatre. Join the crowds in cheering and clapping for eager crooners ranging from giggling 11-year-olds to Broadway-calibre belters.

❺ Falkplatz

Studded with ancient chestnut, oak, birch, ash and poplar trees, this leafy park was a parade ground for Prussian soldiers back in the 19th century and was used to grow vegetables right after WWII. Today, you can watch kids frolicking around the sea-lion fountain.

❻ Burgermania

New York meets Berlin at expat favourite **Bird** (☎030-5105 3283; www.thebirdinberlin.com; Am Falkplatz 5; burgers €10-14.50, steaks from €22.50; ⏰6-11pm Mon-Thu, 4pm-midnight Fri, noon-midnight Sat, noon-11pm Sun; 🛜; 🚋M1, Ⓤ Schönhauser Allee, Ⓢ Schönhauser Allee), whose dry-aged steaks, burgers and hand-cut fries might just justify the hype. Sink your teeth into a dripping half-pounder trapped between a toasted English muffin.

❼ Northern Mauerpark

To escape the Mauerpark frenzy and see where the locals relax, head north of the Gleimstrasse tunnel. This is where you'll find an enchanting birch grove, a farm playground complete with barnyard animals, and a climbing wall.

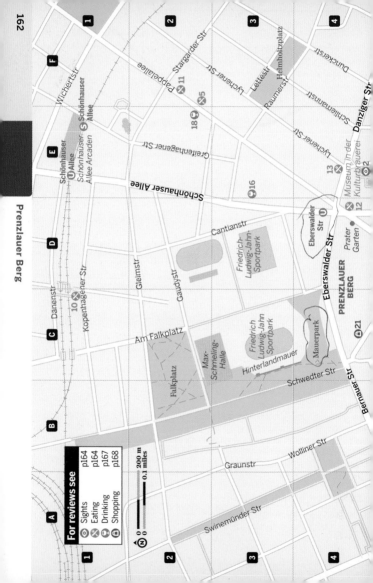

Prenzlauer Berg

For reviews see
◎ Sights	p164
✖ Eating	p164
● Drinking	p167
● Shopping	p168

200 m
0.1 miles

PRENZLAUER
BERG

5

F

8

7

Prenzlauer Allee

Christburger Str

9 15

19 9

22 6

Rykestr

Wörther Str

Husemannstr

Sredzkistr

6

Knaackstr

Belforter Str

Metzer Str

Kollwitzplatz

4

Strassburger Str

Kollwitzstr

Saarbrücker Str

Wörther Str

Kulturbrauerei

10

Jüdischer Friedhof
Schönhauser Allee

3

E

Schönhauser Allee

Schwedter Str

Senefelderplatz

D

Schönhauser Allee

Oderberger Str

Choriner Str

Teutoburger
Platz

Kastanienallee

Schwedter Str

8

Choriner Str

Fehrbelliner Str

7

C

Weinbergsweg

Zionskirchplatz

Arkonaplatz

20

Swinemünder
Str

Fehrbelliner Str

14

Volkspark
Weinberg

Torstr

Wolliner Str

Swinemünder
Str

Veteranenstr

Rosenthaler
Platz

B

Ruppiner str

Brunnenstr

Bernauer Str

Bernauer Str

Bernauer Str

Brunnenstr

5

6

Strelitzer Str

17

Ackerstr

7

8

Sights

Kulturbrauerei
CULTURAL CENTRE

1 ◉ MAP P162, D5

The fanciful red-and-yellow brick buildings of this 19th-century brewery have been upcycled into a cultural powerhouse with a small village's worth of venues, from concert and theatre halls to nightclubs, dance studios, a multiplex cinema and a free GDR history museum. The main entrances are on Knaackstrasse and Sredzkistrasse. (☎030-4435 2170; www.kulturbrauerei.de; btwn Schönhauser Allee, Knaackstrasse, Eberswalder Strasse & Sredzskis-trasse; Ⓟ; 🚊M1, Ⓤ Eberswalder Strasse)

Museum in der Kulturbrauerei
MUSEUM

2 ◉ MAP P162, E4

Original documents, historical footage and objects (including a camper-style Trabi car) bring daily life under socialism in East Germany to life in this government-sponsored exhibit. As you wander the halls, you'll realise the stark contrast between the lofty aspirations of the socialist state and the sobering realities of material shortages, surveillance and oppression its people had to endure. (☎030-467 777 911; www.hdg.de; Knaackstrasse 97; admission free; ⊙10am-6pm Tue, Wed & Fri-Sun, to 8pm Thu; Ⓟ; 🚊M1, 12, Ⓤ Eber-swalder Strasse)

Jüdischer Friedhof Schönhauser Allee
CEMETERY

3 ◉ MAP P162, E6

Berlin's second Jewish cemetery opened in 1827 and hosts many well-known dearly departed, such as the artist Max Liebermann and the composer Giacomo Meyerbeer. It's a pretty place with dappled light filtering through big old chestnuts and linden trees and a sense of mel-ancholy emanating from ivy-draped graves and toppled tombstones. The nicest and oldest have been moved to the Lapidarium by the main entrance. (☎030-441 9824; www.jg-berlin.org; Schönhauser Allee 23-25; ⊙8am-4pm Mon-Thu, 7.30am-2.30pm Fri; Ⓤ Senefelderplatz)

Kollwitzplatz
SQUARE

4 ◉ MAP P162, E6

Triangular Kollwitzplatz was ground zero of Prenzlauer Berg gentrifica-tion. To pick up on the local vibe, linger with macchiato mamas and media daddies in a street cafe or join them at the twice-weekly farmers market (p168). The park in the square's centre is tot heaven with three playgrounds plus a bronze sculpture of the artist Käthe Kollwitz for clambering on. (🚼; Ⓤ Senefelderplatz)

Eating

Mrs Robinson's
INTERNATIONAL €€

5 🍴 MAP P162, F2

When Israel transplant Ben Zviel and his partner Samina Raza launched their minimalist parlour (white-brick walls, polished wooden tables) in 2016, they added another notch to Berlin's food ladder. The menu is constantly in flux, but by turning carefully edited ingredients into shareable small and big plates, Ben fearlessly captures the city's adventurous and uninhibited spirit. Casual fine dining at its best. (☏030-5462 2839, 01520 518 8946; www.mrsrobinsons.de; Pappelallee 29; mains €16-20; ⊗6-11pm Thu-Mon; ☜✎; ☐12, Ⓤ Schönhauser Allee, Ⓢ Schönhauser Allee)

Umami

6 ⊗ MAP P162, F7

VIETNAMESE €

A mellow 1950s lounge vibe and an inspired menu of Indochine home cooking divided into 'regular' and 'vegetarian' choices are the main draws of this restaurant with a large sidewalk terrace. Leave room for their cupcake riff (called 'popcake'). The six-course family meal is a steal at €23 (€10 per additional person). (☏030-2886 0626; www.umami-restaurant.de; Knaackstrasse 16; most mains €7.80; ⊗noon-11pm; ☜✎; ☐M2, Ⓤ Senefelderplatz)

Yafo

ISRAELI €

7 ⊗ MAP P162, C8

This charming resto-bar combo transplants Tel Aviv's palpable energy, sensuous food and convivial vibes to a quiet corner in Berlin. Drop by for a refreshing Aracboy (a cocktail made with Arac, cucumber, lemon and ginger beer) in the buzzy bar or plunge into the eclectically furnished dining room for tahini-drizzled baked

Kulturbrauerei

EZDAN/SHUTTERSTOCK ©

Outdoor Quaffing

Days get long, temperatures climb and spirits soar. Time to celebrate summer beneath the chestnut trees of the **Prater** (Map p162, D4; ☎030-448 5688; www.pratergarten.de; Kastanienallee 7-9; snacks €2.50-7.50; ☉noon-late Apr-Sep, weather permitting; 👶; 🚊M1, 12, Ⓤ Eberswalder Strasse) beer garden or at a sunny cafe on Knaackstrasse or Kastanienallee. Alternatively, score a beverage at a *Späti* (late-hour convenience market) and watch the sunset in the Mauerpark.

cauliflower and other tantalising treats. (☎030-9235 0250; www. yafoberlin.com; Gormannstrasse 17; dishes €6-13; ☉noon-3am; 🛜 🍴; 🚊M8, M10, Ⓤ Rosenthaler Platz, Rosa-Luxemburg-Platz)

W-Der Imbiss
FUSION €

 8 ⊗ MAP P162, C7

The self-described home of 'indo-mexi-cal-ital' fusion, W is always busy as a beehive with fans of its signature naan pizza freshly baked in the tandoor oven and decorated with anything from avocado to smoked salmon. Other standouts are the fish tacos, the thali curry spread and the tandoori salmon. (☎030-4435 2206; www.w-derimbiss. de; Kastanienallee 49; dishes €5-13.50; ☉noon-10pm Sun-Thu, to 11pm Fri & Sat; 🍴; 🚊M1, Ⓤ Rosenthaler Platz)

Chutnify
INDIAN €

9 ⊗ MAP P162, F5

Aparna Aurora's haunt spices up Berlin's bland Indian food scene with authentic South Indian street food. Her specialities are stuffed dosas (a type of savoury rice-flour crêpe) but the curries, biryanis and thali are equally worthy of your attention. (☎030-4401 0795; www. chutnify.com; Sredzkistrasse 43; mains €5-16.50; ☉noon-11pm Tue-Sun; 🍴; 🚊M2, M10, Ⓤ Eberswalder Strasse)

Kanaan
MIDDLE EASTERN €

10 ⊗ MAP P162, C1

In this feel-good venture, an Israeli biz whiz and a Palestinian chef have teamed up to bring vegan/vegetarian Middle Eastern fare to Berlin. Top picks include the Iraqi-style hummus, the *hummshuka* (hummus/shakshouka mash-up) and the chocolate-tahini mousse. Salads are also delish, especially the oven-roasted cauliflower. It's all served in a simple, stylish hut with a lovely garden. (☎0176 2258 6673; www. kanaan-berlin.de; Kopenhagener Strasse 17; dishes €4-10; ☉5-10pm Wed, noon-10pm Thu & Fri, 10am-10pm Sat & Sun; 🛜 🍴; 🚊M1, Ⓤ Schönhauser Allee, Ⓢ Schönhauser Allee)

Zia Maria
ITALIAN €

 11 ⊗ MAP P162, F2

This pizza kitchen and gallery gets a big thumbs-up for its freshly made crispy-crust pizza with classic and eclectic toppings, including wafer-thin prosciutto, nutmeg-laced artichokes and pungent Italian sausage. Vegan and vegetarian varieties are available. Two slices are enough to fill up most bellies. Pour your own wine from the barrel. (www.zia-maria.de; Pappelallee 32a; pizza slices €2-4; ⊙noon-11.30pm; 🚊12, S Schönhauser Allee, U Schönhauser Allee)

Konnopke's Imbiss   GERMAN €

12 🍴 MAP P162, D4

Brave the inevitable queue at this famous sausage kitchen, ensconced in the same spot below the elevated U-Bahn tracks since 1930, but now equipped with a heated pavilion and an English menu. The 'secret' sauce topping is classic *Currywurst* and comes in a four-tier heat scale from mild to wild. (☑030-442 7765; www.konnopke-imbiss.de; Schönhauser Allee 44a; sausages €1.60-2.90; ⊙10am-8pm Mon-Fri, 11.30am-8pm Sat; 🚊M1, M10, M13, U Eberswalder Strasse)

Zum Schusterjungen   GERMAN €€

13 🍴 MAP P162, E4

Tourists, expats and locals descend upon this old-school gastropub where rustic Berlin charm is doled out with as much abandon as the delish home cooking. Big platters of goulash, roast pork and *sauerbraten* feed both tummy and soul, as do the regionally brewed Berliner Schusterjunge pilsner and Märkischer Landmann black beer. (☑030-442 7654; www.zumschusterjungen.com; Danziger Strasse 9; mains €7.50-17; ⊙11am-midnight; U Eberswalder Strasse)

Drinking

Weinerei Forum   WINE BAR

14 MAP P162, B7

After 8pm, this living-room-style cafe turns into a wine bar that works on the honour principle: you 'rent' a wine glass for €2, then help yourself to as much vino as you like and in the end decide what you want to pay. Please be fair to keep this fantastic concept going. (☑030-440 6983; www.weinerei.com; Fehrbelliner Strasse 57; ⊙10am-midnight; 🛜; 🚊M1, U Rosenthaler Platz)

Bryk Bar   COCKTAIL BAR

15 MAP P162, F6

Both vintage and industrial elements contribute to the unhurried, dapper ambience at this darkly lit cocktail lab. Bar chef Frank Grosser whips unusual ingredients into such experimental liquid teasers as the rum-based Kamasutra with a Hangover topped with white chocolate–horseradish foam. The free dill popcorn is positively addictive. (☑030-3810 0165; www.bryk-bar.com; Rykestrasse 18; ⊙7pm-late; 🚊M2, M10, S Prenzlauer Allee)

Zum Starken August   PUB

16 MAP P162, E3

Part circus, part burlesque bar, this venue dressed in Victorian-era exuberance is a fun, friendly addition to the Prenzlauer Berg pub culture. Join the unpretentious crowd over cocktails and craft beers while being entertained with drag-hosted bingo, burlesque divas or wicked cabaret. (📞030-2520 9020; www.zumstarkenaugust.de; Schönhauser Allee 56; ⏰3pm-2.30am Mon-Thu, to 5am Fri, 2pm-5am Sat, 2pm-2.30am Sun; 🚋M1, M10, Ⓤ Eberswalder Strasse)

BrewDog
CRAFT BEER

17 📍 MAP P162, A7

After opening branches around the world, Scottish cult brewers BrewDog are now bringing their fine suds to Berlin. Their modern-industrial flagship with brick walls and dark wood has some 30 taps dispensing their own draughts alongside a changing roster of German and international guest beers. Their pizza pairs well with the amber liquids. (📞030-4847 7770; www.brewdog.com; Ackerstrasse 29; ⏰noon-midnight Sun-Thu, to 2am Fri & Sat; 🚋12, M5, M8, Ⓤ Bernauer Strasse)

Becketts Kopf
COCKTAIL BAR

18 📍 MAP P162, E2

Past Samuel Beckett's portrait, the art of cocktail-making is taken

Kollwitzplatz Market Bounty

On Saturdays, pick up farm-fresh produce and artisanal products before joining locals for gourmet snacks and a glass of bubbly at the colourful **farmers market on Kollwitzplatz** (Kollwitzstrasse & Wörther Strasse; ⏰noon-7pm Thu Apr-Dec, to 6pm Thu Jan-Mar, 9am-4pm Sat; Ⓤ Senefelderplatz).

very seriously. Settle into a heavy armchair in the warmly lit lounge and take your sweet time perusing the extensive – and poetic – drinks menu. All the classics are accounted for, of course, but it's the seasonal special concoctions that truly stimulate the senses. (📞030-9900 5188; www.becketts-kopf.de; Pappelallee 64; ⏰8pm-late; 🚋12, Ⓢ Schönhauser Allee, Ⓤ Schönhauser Allee)

Anna Blume
CAFE

19 📍 MAP P162, F5

Potent java, homemade cakes, and flowers from the attached shop perfume the art nouveau interior of this corner cafe named for a 1919 Dadaist poem by German artist Kurt Schwitters. In fine weather the outdoor terrace offers primo people watching. Great for breakfast (served any time), especially if you order the tiered tray for two. (📞030-4404 8749; www.cafe-anna-blume.de; Kollwitzstrasse 83; breakfast €3.50-12.50, mains €9-13; ⏰8am-midnight; 🚋M2, M10, Ⓤ Eberswalder Strasse)

Shopping

Trödelmarkt Arkonaplatz
MARKET

20 📍 MAP P162, B5

Surrounded by cafes perfect for carbo-loading, this smallish flea market on a leafy square lets you ride the retro frenzy with plenty of groovy furniture, accessories, clothing, vinyl and books, including some East German vintage items. It's easily combined with a visit to the famous Flohmarkt im Mauerpark (p161). (www.troedelmarkt-arkonaplatz.de; Arkonaplatz; ⏱10am-4pm Sun; 🚊M1, M10, ⓊBernauer Strasse)

VEB Orange   GIFTS & SOUVENIRS

21 🔒 MAP P162, C4

Viva vintage! With its selection of the most beautiful things from the '60s and '70s (especially from East Germany), this place is a reminder of how colourful, campy and fun home decor used to be. True to its name, many of the furnishings, accessories, lamps and fashions are orange in colour. (📞030-9788 6886; www.veborange.de; Oderberger Strasse 29; ⏱11am-7pm Mon-Sat; 🚊M1, 12, ⓊEberswalder Strasse)

Saint Georges   BOOKS

22 🔒 MAP P162, F6

Laid-back and low-key, Saint Georges bookshop is a sterling spot to track down new and used English-language fiction and non-

Trödelmarkt Arkonaplatz

fiction. The selection includes plenty of rare and out-of-print books as well as a big shelf of literature by German and international authors translated into English. (📞030-8179 8333; www.saintgeorgesbookshop.com; Wörther Strasse 27; ⏱11am-8pm Mon-Fri, to 7pm Sat; 📶; 🚊M2, ⓊSenefelderplatz)

Worth a Trip 🔭
Schloss & Park Sanssouci

This glorious park-and-palace ensemble is what happens when a king has good taste, plenty of cash and access to the finest architects and artists of the day. Sanssouci was dreamed up by Frederick the Great (1712–86) and is anchored by the eponymous palace, built as a summer retreat in Potsdam, a quick train ride from Berlin. Unesco gave the entire complex World Heritage status in 1990.

📞 0331-969 4200

www.spsg.de

Maulbeerallee

day pass to all palaces adult/concession €19/14

🕐 varies by palace

🚌 606, 695

Schloss Sanssouci

The biggest stunner, and what everyone comes to see, is **Schloss Sanssouci** (adult/concession incl tour or audioguide €12/8; ⊙10am-5.30pm Tue-Sun Apr-Oct, to 5pm Nov & Dec, to 4.30pm Jan-Mar; 🚌614, 650, 695), Frederick the Great's famous summer palace. Designed by Georg Wenzeslaus von Knobelsdorff in 1747, the rococo gem sits daintily above vine-draped terraces with the king's grave nearby.

Standouts on the tours (guided or self-guided) include the **Konzertsaal** (Concert Hall), whimsically decorated with vines, grapes and even a cobweb where sculpted spiders frolic. The king himself gave flute recitals here. Also note the intimate **Bibliothek** (library), lidded by a gilded sunburst ceiling, where the king would seek solace amid 2000 leather-bound tomes ranging from Greek poetry to the latest releases by his friend Voltaire. Another highlight is the **Marmorsaal** (Marble Room), an elegant white Carrara-marble symphony modelled after the Pantheon in Rome.

Chinesisches Haus

The adorable **Chinese House** (Am Grünen Gitter; adult/concession €4/3; ⊙10am-5.30pm Tue-Sun May-Oct; 🚌605, 606, 🚋91) is among the park's most photographed buildings thanks to its enchanting exterior of exotically dressed, gilded figures shown sipping tea, dancing and playing musical instruments amid palm-shaped pillars. Inside is a precious porcelain collection.

Bildergalerie

The **Picture Gallery** (Im Park Sanssouci 4; adult/concession €6/5; ⊙10am-5.30pm Tue-Sun May-Oct; 🚌650, 695) shelters Frederick the Great's prized collection of old masters, including such pearls as Caravaggio's *Doubting Thomas*, Anthony van Dyck's *Pentecost* and several

★ Top Tips

o Book your timed ticket to Schloss Sanssouci online to avoid wait times and/or disappointment.

o Avoid visiting on Monday when most palaces are closed.

o The sanssouci+ ticket, a one-day pass to palaces in Potsdam, costs €19 (concession €14) and is sold online and at each building.

✕ Take a Break

For international favourites, head to **Potsdam Zur Historischen Mühle** (📞0331-281 493; Zur Historischen Mühle 2; mains €11-20; ⊙8am-10pm; 🅿 👶; 🚌614, 650, 695); it has a beer garden and children's playground.

★ Getting There

Potsdam is 24km southwest of the city centre.

🚆 It's 25 minutes from Berlin Hauptbahnhof or Zoologischer Garten to Potsdam Hauptbahnhof.

Ⓢ The S7 takes 40 minutes.

works by Peter Paul Rubens. Behind the rather plain facade hides a sumptuous arrangement of gilded ornamentation, yellow and white marble and a patterned stone floor that is perhaps just as impressive as the mostly large-scale paintings that cover practically every inch of wall space.

Neues Palais

The final palace commissioned by Frederick the Great, the **Neues Palais** (New Palace; Am Neuen Palais; adult/concession incl tour or audio-guide €8/6; ⊙10am-5.30pm Mon & Wed-Sun Apr-Oct, to 5pm Nov-Dec, to 4.30pm Jan-Mar; 🚌605, 606, 695, ⓢPotsdam Charlottenhof) has made-to-impress dimensions, a central dome and a lavish exterior capped with a parade of sandstone figures. After extensive restoration, most

of the building's highlights are once again accessible, including the shell-festooned **Grottensaal** (Grotto Hall) festival hall and the magnificent **Marmorsaal** (Marble Hall), where visitors walk across a raised pathway to protect the precious marble floor illuminated by eight massive crystal chandeliers. Also looking splendid is the redone **Unteres Fürstenquartier** (Lower Royal Suite), which consists of a concert room, an oval-shaped chamber, an antechamber and, most impressively, a dining room with walls sheathed in red silk damask with gold-braided trim.

Orangerieschloss

Modelled after an Italian Renaissance villa, the 300m-long, 1864-built **Orangery Palace** (An der Orangerie 3-5; adult/concession €6/5,

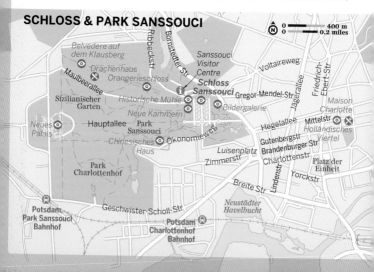

SCHLOSS & PARK SANSSOUCI

0 ——— 400 m
0 ——— 0.2 miles

Belvedere auf dem Klausberg
Drachenhaus
Maulbeerallee
Ribbeckstr
Bornstedter Str
Orangerieschloss
Sanssouci Visitor Centre
Voltaireweg
Friedrich-Ebert-Str
Historische Mühle
Schloss Sanssouci
Gregor-Mendel-Str
Sizilianischer Garten
Neue Kammern
Bildergalerie
Maison Charlotte
Neues Palais
Hauptallee
Park Sanssouci
Hegelallee
Mittelstr
Hollandisches Viertel
Chinesisches Haus
Ökonomieweg
Gutenbergstr
Brandenburger Str
Luisenplatz
Zimmerstr
Charlottenstr
Platz der Einheit
Park Charlottenhof
Lindenstr
Yorckstr
Breite Str
Neustädter Havelbucht
Potsdam, Park Sanssouci Bahnhof
Geschwister-Scholl-Str
Potsdam Charlottenhof Bahnhof

tower €3/2; ⊙10am-5.30pm Tue-Sun May-Oct, 10am-5.30pm Sat & Sun Apr; 🚌695) was the favourite building project of Friedrich Wilhelm IV – a passionate Italophile. Its highlight is the **Raffaelsaal** (Raphael Hall), which brims with 19th-century copies of the famous painter's masterpieces.

Neue Kammern

The **New Chambers** (adult/concession incl tour or audioguide €6/5; ⊙10am-5.30pm Tue-Sun Apr-Oct; 🚌614, 650, 695), built by Knobelsdorff in 1748, were originally an orangery and later converted into a guest palace. The interior drips with rococo opulence, most notably the square **Jasper Hall**, which is drenched in precious stones and lidded by a Venus fresco, and the **Ovidsaal**, a grand ballroom with gilded wall reliefs depicting scenes from Ovid's *Metamorphosis*.

Schloss Charlottenhof

This small **palace** (Geschwister-Scholl-Strasse 34a; tours adult/concession €6/5; ⊙tours 10am-5.30pm Tue-Sun May-Oct; 🚌605, 606, 610, X5, 🚊91, 94, 98) started out as a baroque country manor before being expanded by Karl Friedrich Schinkel for Friedrich Wilhelm IV in the late 1820s. The building is modelled on classical Roman villas and features a Doric portico and a bronze fountain.

Historische Mühle

This reconstructed 18th-century Dutch-style **windmill** (📞0331-550 6851; www.spsg.de; Maulbeerallee 5; adult/concession €4/3; ⊙10am-6pm daily Apr-Oct, to 4pm Sat & Sun Nov & Jan-Mar; 🅿; 🚌650, 695) contains exhibits about the history of the mill and mill technology, and offers a close-up look at the grinding mechanism and a top-floor viewing platform.

Nearby: Museum Barberini

The original **Barberini Palace** (www.museum-barberini.com; Alter Markt, Humboldtstrasse 5-6; adult/concession/under 18 €14/10/free; ⊙10am-7pm Wed-Mon, 1st Thu of month to 9pm; 🚌91, 92, 93, 96, 99 Alter Markt/Landtag) was a baroque Roman palazzo commissioned by Frederick the Great and bombed to bits in World War II. Since January 2017, a majestic replica houses a private art museum that mounts three high-calibre exhibits per year with an artistic arc that spans East German works, old masters and modern greats such as Gerhard Richter.

Survival Guide

Potsdamer Platz (p76) RICOWDE/GETTY IMAGES ©

Before You Go

Book Your Stay

○ Berlin has over 142,000 hotel rooms but the most desirable properties book up quickly, especially in summer and around major holidays, festivals and trade shows; prices soar and reservations are essential during these periods.

○ Otherwise, rates are mercifully low by Western capital standards. Options range from luxurious ports of call to ho-hum international chains, trendy designer boutique hotels to Old Berlin–style B&Bs, happening hostels to handy self-catering apartments.

○ The most central district is Mitte. Hotels around Kurfürstendamm are plentiful but put you an *U-Bahn* ride away from most blockbuster sights and nightlife.

○ Lodging in Kreuzberg and Friedrichshain is handy for party animals.

○ Berlin's hostel scene is as vibrant as ever with

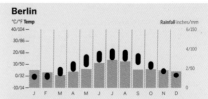

Berlin
°C/°F Temp
Rainfall inches/mm

When to Go

○ **Winter (Nov–Feb)**
Cold and dark, snow possible. Sights are crowd-free; theatre and concert season in full swing.

○ **Spring (Mar–May)**
Mild, often sunny. Sights start getting busier; festival season starts; beer gardens and outdoor cafes open.

○ **Summer (Jun–Aug)**
Warm to hot, often sunny, thunderstorms possible. Peak tourist season; sights and museums are super-busy; life moves outdoors.

○ **Autumn (Sep–Oct)**
Mild, often sunny. Theatre, concert and football (soccer) seasons start up.

dorms beds available for as little as €10.

Useful Websites

○ **Lonely Planet** (lonelyplanet.com/germany/hotels) Lonely Planet's online booking service with insider low-down on the best places to stay.

○ **Visit Berlin** (www.visitberlin.de) Official Berlin tourist office; books rooms at partner hotels with a best-price guarantee.

○ **Boutique Hotels Berlin** (www.boutique

hotels-berlin.com) Booking service for hand-picked boutique hotels.

○ **Berlin30** (www.berlin30.com) Low-cost booking agency for hotels, hostels, apartments and B&Bs in Berlin.

Best Budget

Grand Hostel Berlin Classic (www.grandhostel-berlin.de) Connect to the magic of yesteryear at this historic lair imbued with both character and modern amenities.

Wombat's Berlin
(www.wombats-hostels.
com/berlin) Fun seek-
ers should thrive at this
well-run hostel with hip
in-house bar.

**EastSeven Berlin
Hostel** (www.east
seven.de) Friendly and
low-key hostel with
communal vibe ideal
for solo travellers.

Circus Hostel (www.
circus-berlin.de)This
classic is a superb
launch pad for fun-
seekers and culture
cravers.

Plus Berlin (www.plus
hostels.com/plusberlin)
Next-gen hostel with
pool in stumbling
distance of bar and club
central in Friedrichshain.

Best Midrange

Circus Hotel (www.
circus-berlin.de) Peren-
nial pleaser thanks to
being a perfect synthe-
sis of style, comfort,
location and value.

Orania Hotel (www.
orania.berlin) Culturally
minded style pad with
superb restaurant and
live concerts.

**Adina Apartment Hotel
Berlin Checkpoint
Charlie** (www.adina
hotels.com) Ideal base
for budget-conscious,

space-craving self-
caterers.

Michelberger Hotel
(www.michelberger
hotel.com) Zeitgeist-
capturing crash pad
with funky industrial DIY
aesthetics and popular
restaurant.

**25hours Hotel Bikini
Berlin** (www.25hours-
hotels.com) Inner-city
playground with easy
access to top shopping
and rooms overlooking
the Berlin Zoo.

Best Top End

Mandala Hotel (www.
themandala.de) All-
suite city slicker with
uncluttered urban feel
and top eats.

Hotel am Steinplatz
(www.hotelsteinplatz.
com) Art-deco jewel
with top-notch bar and
restaurant.

Hotel de Rome (www.
roccofortehotels.com)
Posh player in a former
bank building with
rooftop bar and bank-
vault spa.

Das Stue (www.das-
stue.com) Charismatic
refuge from the urban
bustle with understated
grandeur and the
Tiergarten park as a
front yard.

Bed Tax
Value-added
tax (VAT; 7%)
has long been
included in room
rates, but since
1 January 2014
an additional 5%
'city tax' is added
to the net room
rates, eg exclud-
ing VAT and fees
for amenities and
services. Busi-
ness travellers
are exempt from
this tax.

Arriving in Berlin

Tegel Airport

○ About 8km northwest
of Zoologischer Garten
and 13km northwest of
Alexanderplatz, **Tegel
Airport** (TXL; ☎030-6091
1150; www.berlin-airport.
de; ☒Flughafen Tegel) is
Berlin's main airport.

○ The TXL express
bus connects Tegel to
Alexanderplatz (40 min-
utes) via Hauptbahnhof
(central train station)
and Unter den Linden
every 10 minutes. Buses

stop outside the main entrance to Terminal A.

o The closest *S-Bahn* station is Jungfernheide (S41/S42 or *Ringbahn*, or circle line). Linked to the airport by bus X9.

o The closest *U-Bahn* station is Jakob-Kaiser-Platz, which is connected by bus 109 and X9 to the airport. From Jakob-Kaiser-Platz, the U7 goes to Schöneberg, Kreuzberg and Neukölln.

o All journeys cost €2.80 (Tariff AB).

o Taxi rides cost about €25 to Zoologischer Garten and €28 to Alexanderplatz and take 30 to 45 minutes. A €0.50 surcharge applies to trips from this airport.

Schönefeld Airport

o About 22km southeast of Alexanderplatz, **Schönefeld Airport** (SXF; ☏030-6091 1150; www.berlin-airport.de; ⓡAirport-Express, RE7 & RB14, Ⓢ S9, S45) is served by *S-Bahn* and regional trains.

o The airport train station is 400m from the terminals; free shuttle buses run every 10 minutes.

o Airport-Express trains (denoted as RE7 and RB14 in timetables) travel to central Berlin twice hourly (20 to 30 minutes). The slower S-Bahn S9 train departs every 20 minutes.

o Buy tickets from vending machines in the station tunnel and on platforms (EC cards and cash; change given) and validate them before boarding.

o The nearest *U-Bahn* station, Rudow, is served by the U7 and about a 10-minute ride on bus X7 or bus 171 from the airport. It's useful for travel to Neukölln or Kreuzberg.

o All journeys cost €3.40 (ABC tariff).

o Cabs to central Berlin need about an hour and cost €45 to €50.

Hauptbahnhof (Central Train Station)

o Berlin's central train station is just north of the Reichstag and Brandenburg Gate and is served by the *U-Bahn*, the *S-Bahn*, trams and buses.

o Taxi ranks are located outside the north exit

(Europaplatz) and the south exit (Washington-platz).

o The left-luggage office (€5 per piece, per 24 hours) is behind the Reisebank currency exchange on level OG1, opposite the Reisezentrum.

Zentraler Omnibus Bahnhof (ZOB, Central Coach Station)

o The newly upgraded **Zentraler Omnibus-bahnhof** (ZOB, Central Bus Station; ☏030-3010 0175; www.zob-berlin.de; Messedamm 8; Ⓢ Messe/ ICC Nord, Ⓤ Kaiserdamm) is near the trade fairgrounds on the western city edge. Flixbus also stops at around a dozen other points in town, including the airports and Alexanderplatz.

o The closest *U-Bahn* station to ZOB is Kaiserdamm, about 400m north and served by the U2 line, which travels through the city centre. Tickets cost €2.80 (Tariff AB).

o The nearest *S-Bahn* station is Messe Süd/ ICC, about 200m east of

ZOB. It is served by the Ringbahn (circle line) S41/S42 and handy for such districts as Prenzlauer Berg, Friedrichshain and Neukölln. You need an AB ticket (€2.80).

o Budget about €14 for a taxi ride to the western city centre around Zoo station and €24 to the eastern city centre around Alexanderplatz.

Getting Around

U-Bahn

o The *U-Bahn* is the quickest way of getting around Berlin.

o Lines (referred to as U1, U2 etc) operate from 4am until about 12.30am and throughout the night on Friday, Saturday and public holidays (all lines except the U4 and U55).

o From Sunday to Thursday, night buses take over in the interim.

S-Bahn

o *S-Bahn* trains (S1, S2 etc) don't run as frequently as the *U-Bahn*,

but they make fewer stops and are thus useful for covering longer distances.

o Trains operate from 4am to 12.30am and all night on Friday, Saturday and public holidays.

Bus

o Buses run frequently between 4.30am and 12.30am.

o Night buses (N19, N23 etc) take over after 12.30am.

o MetroBuses, designated M19, M41 etc, operate 24/7.

Tram

o Trams (*Strassenbahn*) operate almost exclusively in the eastern districts.

o Trams designated M1, M2 etc run 24/7.

Bicycle

o Bicycles may be taken aboard designated *U-Bahn* and *S-Bahn* carriages (look for the bicycle logo) as well as on night buses (Sunday to Thursday only) and trams.

o You need a separate bicycle ticket called a *Fahrradkarte* (€1.90).

Taxi

o You can order a **taxi** (☏030-210 202, 030-443 322, 030-210 101; www.taxi-in-berlin.de) by phone, flag one down or pick one up at a rank. At night, cars often wait outside theatres, clubs and other venues.

o Flag fall is €3.90, then it's €2 per kilometre up to 7km and €1.50 for each additional kilometre.

o There's a surcharge of €1.50 if paying by credit or debit card.

o Tip about 10%.

o The *Kurzstreckentarif* (short-trip rate) lets you ride in a cab for up to 2km for €5 provided you flag down a moving taxi and request this rate before boarding.

Essential Information

Accessible Travel

o Access ramps and/or lifts are available in many public buildings, including train stations and museums.

Tickets & Passes

○ One ticket is valid for all forms of public transport.

○ The network comprises fare zones A, B and C with tickets available for zones AB, BC or ABC.

○ AB tickets, valid for two hours, cover most city trips (interruptions and transfers allowed, but round-trips are not). Exceptions: Potsdam and Schönefeld Airport (ABC tariff).

○ Children aged six to 14 qualify for reduced (ermässigt) rates; kids under six travel free.

○ Buy tickets from bus drivers, vending machines at *U-Bahn* or *S-Bahn* stations, and aboard trams, and at station offices and news kiosks sporting the yellow BVG logo. Some vending machines accept debit cards. Bus drivers and tram vending machines only take cash.

○ Single tickets, except those bought from bus drivers and in trams, must be validated at station platform entrances.

○ On-the-spot fine for travelling without a valid ticket: €60.

○ A range of travel passes offer better value than single tickets.

○ Most buses, trains and trams are wheelchair-accessible and many *U-Bahn* and *S-Bahn* stations are equipped with ramps or lifts. For trip-planning assistance, contact the **BVG** (☎ 030-194 49; www.bvg.de).

○ For a databank assessing the accessibility of cafes, restaurants, hotels, theatres and other public spaces (in German), check with Mobidat (www.mobidat.de).

Business Hours

The following are typical opening hours, although these may vary seasonally and by location (city centre or the suburbs).

Bars 7pm–1am or later

Boutiques 11am–7pm Monday–Friday, to 6pm Saturday

Cafes 8am–8pm

Clubs 11pm–5am or later

Restaurants 11am–11pm

Shops 10am–8pm Monday–Saturday

Supermarkets 8am–8pm or later; some 24 hours

Discount Cards

Berlin Welcome Card (www.berlin-welcome card.de) Valid for unlimited public transport for one adult and up to three children under 14; up to 50% discount to 200 sights, attractions and tours; available for up to six days.

CityTourCard (www. citytourcard.com) Similar to the Berlin Welcome Card but a bit cheaper and with fewer discounts.

Museumspass Berlin (adult/concession €29/14.50) Buys

admission to the permanent exhibits of about 30 museums for three consecutive days. Sold at tourist offices and participating museums.

Electricity

Type C
220V/50Hz

Emergencies

Ambulance	☏112
Fire department	☏112
Police	☏110

Money

○ Cash is king in Germany.

○ ATMs (*Geldautomat*) are the best and easiest way to get cash. Most are accessible 24/7.

○ Credit cards are becoming more widely accepted (especially in hotels and upmarket shops and restaurants), but it's best to enquire first.

○ Some places require a minimum purchase with credit card use.

Public Holidays

Shops, banks and public and private offices are closed on the following nationwide *gesetzliche Feiertage* (public holidays):

Neujahrstag (New Year's Day) 1 January

Ostern (Easter) March/April; Good Friday, Easter Sunday and Easter Monday

Christi Himmelfahrt (Ascension Day) Forty days after Easter, always on a Thursday

Maifeiertag (Labour Day) 1 May

Pfingsten (Whitsun/Pentecost Sunday and Monday) May/June

Tag der Deutschen Einheit (Day of German Unity) 3 October

Weihnachtstag (Christmas Day) 25 December

Zweiter Weihnachtstag (Boxing Day) 26 December

Telephone

○ Berlin's city code is ☏030; Germany's country code is ☏49.

○ Mobile phones operate on GSM900/1800.

○ Local SIM cards can be used in unlocked European and Australian phones.

○ US multiband phones also work in Germany.

Late Night & Sunday Shopping

○ One handy feature of Berlin culture is the *Spätkauf* (*Späti* in local vernacular), which are small neighbourhood stores stocked with the basics and open until 2am or later.

○ Some supermarkets stay open until midnight; a few are open 24 hours.

○ Shops and supermarkets in major train stations (Hauptbahnhof, Ostbahnhof, Friedrichstrasse) are open late and on Sunday.

Do's & Don'ts

o Do say 'Guten Tag' when entering a business.

o Do state your last name at the start of a phone call.

o Do bring a small gift or flowers when invited to a home-cooked meal.

o Bring a bag to shop at supermarkets and pack your own groceries.

o Don't be late for appointments and dinner invitations.

o Don't assume you can pay by credit card, especially when eating out.

Tourist Information

Visit Berlin (www. visitberlin.de), the Berlin tourist board, operates five walk-in offices, info desks at the airports, and a **call centre** (🕿030-2500 2333; 🕙9am-6pm Mon-Fri) whose multilingual staff field general questions and make hotel and ticket bookings.

Alexanderplatz

(🕿030-250 025; www. visitberlin.de; lobby Park Inn, Alexanderplatz 7; 🕙7am-9pm Mon-Sat,

8am-6pm Sun; 🚌100, 200, TXL, Ⓤ Alexander-platz, Ⓢ Alexanderplatz)

Brandenburger Tor

(🕿030-250 023; www. visitberlin.de; Pariser Platz, Brandenburger Tor, south wing; 🕙9.30am-7pm Apr-Oct, to 6pm Nov-Mar; Ⓢ Brandenburger Tor, Ⓤ Brandenburger Tor)

Central Bus Station (ZOB) (www.visitberlin. de; Masurenallee 4-6; 🕙8am-8pm Mon, Fri & Sat, to 4pm Tue-Thu & Sun; Ⓢ Messe Nord/ICC)

Europa-Center (🕿030-2500 2333; www.visitberlin. de; Tauentzienstrasse 9,

Europa-Center, ground fl; 🕙10am-8pm Mon-Sat; 🚌100, 200, Ⓤ Kurfürsten-damm, Zoologischer Garten, Ⓢ Zoologischer Garten)

Hauptbahnhof

(🕿030-250 025; www. visitberlin.de; Hauptbahn-hof, Europaplatz entrance, ground fl; 🕙8am-10pm; Ⓢ Hauptbahnhof, Ⓡ Hauptbahnhof)

Visas

o EU nationals need only their national identity card or passport to enter Germany.

o Citizens of Australia, Canada, Israel, Japan, New Zealand, Switzer-land and the US are among those who need only a valid passport (no visa) if entering as tourists for a stay of up to three months within a six-month period.

o Nationals from other countries need a Schengen Visa to enter Germany. Check with a German consulate in your country.

Language

It's easy to pronounce German because almost all sounds are also found in English – just read our pronunciation guides as if they were English and you'll be understood.

In German, word stress falls mostly on the first syllable – in our pronunciation guides the stressed syllable is indicated with italics.

Note that German has polite and informal forms for 'you' (*Sie* and *du* respectively). When addressing people you don't know well, use the polite form. In this language guide, polite forms are used, unless you see (pol/inf) which indicates we've given both options. Also note that (m/f) indicates masculine and feminine forms.

To enhance your trip with a phrasebook, visit **lonelyplanet.com**.

Basics

Hello.
Guten Tag. goo·ten taak

Goodbye.
Auf owf
Wiedersehen. vee·der·zey·en

How are you? (pol/inf)
Wie geht es vee gayt es
Ihnen/dir? ee·nen/deer

Fine, thanks.
Danke, gut. dang·ke goot

Please.
Bitte. bi·te

Thank you.
Danke. dang·ke

Excuse me.
Entschuldigung. ent·shul·di·gung

Sorry.
Entschuldigung. ent·shul·di·gung

Yes./No.
Ja./Nein. yah/nain

Do you speak (English)?
Sprechen Sie shpre·khen zee
Englisch? eng·lish

I (don't) understand.
Ich verstehe ikh fer·shtay·e
(nicht). (nikht)

Eating & Drinking

I'm a vegetarian. (m/f)
Ich bin Vegetarier/ ikh bin ve·ge·
 tah·ri·er/
Vegetarierin. ve·ge·tah·ri·e·in

Cheers!
Prost! prawst

That was delicious!
Das war sehr das vahr zair
lecker! le·ker

Please bring the bill.
Die Rechnung, dee rekh·nung
bitte. bi·te

I'd like ...
Ich möchte ... ikh merkh·te ...

a coffee *einen Kaffee* ai·nen ka·fay

a glass of *ein Glas* ain glas
wine *Wein* wain

a table *einen Tisch* ai·nen tish
for two *für zwei* für tsvai
 Personen per·zaw·nen

two beers *zwei Bier* tsvai beer

Shopping

I'd like to buy ...
Ich möchte ... ikh merkh·te ...
kaufen. kow·fen

May I look at it?
Können Sie es ker·nen zee es
mir zeigen? meer tsai·gen

How much is it?
Wie viel kostet das? vee feel kos·tet das

That's too expensive.
Das ist zu teuer. das ist tsoo *toy*·er

Can you lower the price?
Können Sie mit *ker*·nen zee mit
dem Preis dem prais
heruntergehen? he·*run*·ter·gay·en

There's a mistake in the bill.
Da ist ein Fehler in dah ist ain *fay*·ler in
der Rechnung. dair *rekh*·nung

Emergencies

Help!
Hilfe! *hil*·fe

Call a doctor!
Rufen Sie *roo*·fen zee
einen Arzt! *ai*·nen artst

Call the police!
Rufen Sie *roo*·fen zee
die Polizei! dee po·li·*tsai*

I'm lost.
Ich habe ikh *hah*·be
mich verirrt. mikh fer·*irt*

I'm ill.
Ich bin krank. ikh bin krangk

Where's the toilet?
Wo ist die Toilette? vo ist dee to·a·*le*·te

Time & Numbers

What time is it?
Wie spät ist es? vee shpayt ist es

It's (10) o'clock.
Es ist (zehn) Uhr. es ist (tsayn) oor

morning	*Morgen*	*mor*·gen
afternoon	*Nach-mittag*	*nahkh-mi*·tahk
evening	*Abend*	*ah*·bent
yesterday	*gestern*	*ges*·tern
today	*heute*	*hoy*·te
tomorrow	*morgen*	*mor*·gen

1	*eins*	ains
2	*zwei*	tsvai
3	*drei*	drai
4	*vier*	feer
5	*fünf*	fünf
6	*sechs*	zeks
7	*sieben*	zee·ben
8	*acht*	akht
9	*neun*	noyn
10	*zehn*	tsayn
100	*hundert*	hun·dert
1000	*tausend*	tow·sent

Transport & Directions

Where's ...?
Wo ist ...? vaw ist ...

What's the address?
Wie ist die vee ist dee
Adresse? a·*dre*·se

Can you show me (on the map)?
Können Sie es mir *ker*·nen zee es meer
(auf der Karte) (owf dair *kar*·te)
zeigen? *tsai*·gen

I want to go to ...
Ich mochte ikh *merkh*·te
nach ... fahren. nahkh ... *fah*·ren

What time does it leave?
Wann fährt es ab? van fairt es ap

What time does it arrive?
Wann kommt van komt
es an? es an

Does it stop at ...?
Hält es in ...? helt es in ...

I want to get off here.
Ich mochte hier ikh *merkh*·te heer
aussteigen. ows·*shtai*·gen

Behind the Scenes

Send Us Your Feedback

We love to hear from travellers – your comments help make our books better. We read every word, and we guarantee that your feedback goes straight to the authors. Visit **lonelyplanet.com/contact** to submit your updates and suggestions.

Note: We may edit, reproduce and incorporate your comments in Lonely Planet products such as guidebooks, websites and digital products, so let us know if you don't want your comments reproduced or your name acknowledged. For a copy of our privacy policy visit lonelyplanet.com/privacy.

Andrea's Thanks

Big heartfelt thanks to all of the wonderful people who plied me with tips, insights, information, ideas and encouragement (in no particular order): Henrik Tidefjärd, Barbara Woolsey, Tina Engler, Kerstin Riedel, Regine Schneider, Shaul Margulies, Frank Engster, Heiner and Claudia Schuster, Bernd Olsson, Tina Schürmann, Claudia Scheffler, Kirsten Schmidt, Renate Freiling, Tatjana Debel-Smykalla, David Eckel, Shachar and Doreen Elkanati, Nora Durstewitz and, of course, David Peevers.

Acknowledgements

Cover photograph: Berliner Dom and Spree River, Sabine Lubenow/ AWL ©
Photographs pp34-5 (from left): Sergey Kelin; S-F; Aleksandar Todorovic; Di Gregorio Giulio; turtix / Shutterstock ©

This Book

This 6th edition of Lonely Planet's *Pocket Berlin* guidebook was researched and written by Andrea Schulte-Peevers, who also wrote the previous two editions. This guidebook was produced by the following:

Destination Editor
Niamh O'Brien

Senior Product Editor
Genna Patterson

Product Editor
Joel Cotterell

Senior Cartographer
Valentina Kremenchutskaya

Book Designer
Mazzy Prinsep

Assisting Editors James Bainbridge, Gabrielle Innes, Rosie Nicholson, Tamara Sheward, Gabrielle Stefanos

Cover Researcher
Naomi Parker

Thanks to Lili Helena Duchow, Wayne Murphy, Jenna Myers, Claire Naylor, Karyn Noble, Martine Power

Index

See also separate subindexes for:

- ⊗ **Eating p188**
- ⊕ **Drinking p189**
- ⊕ **Entertainment p190**
- ⊕ **Shopping p190**

Sights 000
Map Pages **000**

Our Writer

Andrea Schulte-Peevers

Born and raised in Germany and educated in London and at UCLA, Andrea has travelled the distance to the moon and back in her visits to some 75 countries. She has earned her living as a professional travel writer for more than two decades and authored or contributed to nearly 100 Lonely Planet titles as well as to newspapers, magazines and websites around the world. She also works as a travel consultant, translator and editor. Andrea's destination expertise is especially strong when it comes to Germany, Dubai and the UAE, Crete and the Caribbean Islands. She makes her home in Berlin.

Published by Lonely Planet Global Limited
CRN 554153
6th edition – Feb 2019
ISBN 978 1 78657 798 6
© Lonely Planet 2019   Photographs © as indicated 2019
10 9 8 7 6 5 4 3 2 1
Printed in Singapore